Chinese Girl in the Ghetto

Chinese Girl in the Ghetto

Ying Ma

Grateful acknowledgement is made to the following for permission to reprint previously published material:

FrontPageMag.com: Excerpts from "Ghetto Racism," by Ying Ma. Reprinted from FrontPageMag.com.

Dow Jones & Company, Inc.: Excerpts from "China, 1984," by Ying Ma. Reprinted from The Wall Street Journal Asia © 2011 Dow Jones & Company, Inc. All rights reserved.

ISBN-13: 978-146097045-4

Printed in the United States of America

To my parents and my brother

Author's Note

The names of the individuals who figure in this book's stories have been altered to protect their privacy. Many of the dialogues recounted here are approximations of those that took place many years ago. I have retold these stories from my childhood and adolescence to the best of my ability and have confirmed the relevant facts with my family wherever possible. Regardless, memory is not perfect, so any factual mistakes in the text remain my responsibility.

Contents

Introduction

When I started writing this book, I told myself—and anyone who asked—that it was about freedom. Although I was writing about my journey from Guangzhou, China's third-largest city, to inner-city Oakland, California, I described the book as a chronicle of a journey from authoritarianism to a free society, a story about freedom.

Certainly, I did not conjure this description out of thin air. I was writing about daily life in post-Mao China, where economic reforms were rapidly transforming the country into a more hopeful, more colorful place, even though the hand of the state continued to intrude into its citizens' lives insidiously and ominously. I was also writing about the horrors of inner-city America and the disappointment of scraping by at the bottom of a free society.

However, I was never able to fully convince myself that freedom was really what the book was about. Much as I wished to deny or deemphasize it, this book offered stories about my life, my perceptions, and my decisions. Yet admitting that I was writing a book about myself seemed awfully narcissistic, especially since my list of accomplishments is short, my name recognition nonexistent. Having written opinion-editorials for newspapers and articles for policy magazines for more than a decade, I was also keenly aware of how public policy issues related to my childhood and teenage experiences in China and the United States. As such, I felt the need to insert policy observations into my personal stories. Repeatedly, I reminded myself that my stories shed light not just on my life, but on important issues such as promoting freedom abroad or improving racial relations at home.

Then the year 2010 arrived and brought forth multiple crimes that forced me to look at my book project in a wholly different light.

In April, two black teenagers punched a Chinese immigrant, 59-year-old Tian Sheng Yu, in the mouth in downtown Oakland. He fell on his head, spent the next few days in critical care, and subsequently died. The same two teenagers assaulted the victim's 27-year-old son before *and* after they assaulted the father. Between late March and early April of the same year, five black teenagers assailed five older Asian women, including one who was 71 years old, on separate occasions in or near a public housing project on the Lower East Side of New York City. In late March, five black teenagers surrounded a 57-year-old Asian woman at a light rail bus stop in San Francisco; one of them grabbed her and threw her from the platform onto the rails before beating her. In January, black teenagers kicked and beat 83-year-old Huan Chen after he got off the same bus stop. He, too, died from his injuries.

Some of the perpetrators, like those who attacked

Mr. Huan Chen, demanded money before they ran off laughing. Most, however, acted for no apparent reason aside from the satisfaction of perpetrating a beating.

After the attacks, an uncomfortable question stared everyone in the face: What role had racism played in motivating the attacks? In response, local officials and local media bent over backwards to deny or discount the issue of race. Former San Francisco Supervisor Sophie Maxwell eagerly labeled the attackers as mere thugs who targeted the "weak and vulnerable," while San Francisco Police Chief George Gascon insisted that the attacks against Asians were mere "crimes of opportunity," not incidents of racial targeting. Then Oakland City Council member and current Oakland Mayor Jean Quan blamed the Chinese residents of her city for making themselves "easier targets" through their frequent failure to report crimes committed against them. Meanwhile, New York City's mainstream local media sources, including WCBS and NBC New York, failed to report the race of the five teenagers who terrorized the elderly Asian women on the Lower East Side, even though the perpetrators' race was there for the world to see, on surveillance video.

Had white teenagers inflicted similarly horrific violence on Asian residents across America in a series of incidents over a four-month period, the country—or at least the cities where the crimes took place—would have rushed to engage in serious soul-searching about white attitudes toward Asians. Where black-on-Asian violence was concerned, however, America's fear of confronting painful truths beyond the bounds of political correctness became all too clear.

As news about the sadistic attacks hit the Internet and airwaves, I quickly lost interest in inserting commentary about freedom into my draft chapters. The ghetto ceased to be a memory that I recounted on a computer screen. Instead, it came alive on the pained faces of every victim who suffered an attack or lost a loved one. I watched the widow of the late Tian Sheng Yu, who was attacked and killed in Oakland, appear on television with her eyes swollen, bravely trying to speak about her loss. Justice, she told reporters in Mandarin, would prevail if what happened to her family did not ever happen to anyone else. Without hesitation, she added that she truly regretted coming to America.

During this time, I remembered the face of the ghetto vividly—the ever-present threat of violence, the constant racism, the never-ending poverty, the all-consuming hopelessness of urban decay. I also remembered the customary eagerness with which many Americans look away from the ghetto's tragedies as they make excuses for the behavior of individuals who inflict harm.

In the end, my memories of the ghetto's ugliness fueled the completion of this book. Instead of writing a book about domestic and foreign policy, I have written a memoir about my childhood and adolescence and the journey through which I morphed from a carefree and happy child living under post-Mao Chinese authoritarianism to a bitter, foul-mouthed teenager fighting against the shadows of the American inner city. I have tried to recount my stories from Guangzhou with the fondness and tenderness that the city deserves, and I have told my stories about the ghetto with every bit of the anger that it instilled in me.

I know that I am not the only one who has stories from the ghetto. Though the details may be different, my stories are also the stories of numerous others who have endured the same indignities, encountered the same crimes, felt the same rage, and struggled to break away from the same ugliness. I know because you have written to me after reading my articles on this subject. You shared your own experiences, and in your anger and humiliation, I recognized my own. In each of my stories about the ghetto, I saw you—every elderly Asian person who has ever walked down the streets of urban America alone, afraid, and unable to speak English; every Asian schoolchild who has run away from or remained silent before racist thugs because she was nerdy and smaller in size; and every Asian adult immigrant who has seen his hard-earned cash or possessions taken away by force but was helpless to defend himself and unable to obtain protection from the law.

But these were not the only faces I saw. I also saw the faces of the worst victims of the ghetto's brokenness, many of whom shared the same skin color as those who perpetrated crimes against them. I saw the hate, the self-loathing, and the self-destruction that grow when a people have been wronged by history and when an individual believes he will be no exception. I concurred with Mrs. Yu, when days after her husband's death, she conveyed to the congregation of a large black church in Oakland that "we are one family."

This belief guided the writing of this book. In Guangzhou, I could not avoid the randomness, the ambiguity, or the all-encompassing weight of authoritarianism, but in the loving embrace of my family and the unflinching loyalty of my friends, I remained upbeat, cheerful, and happy. In the ghetto, I forgot what it meant to be joyful. But even in the ghetto, people have a chance to walk away from some of the worst attributes of a free society into its finest virtues, and they have a choice to believe that all Americans, however different, can be "one family." It is this belief that lies at the heart of my journey of getting to know freedom, and I hope it shines through the hate of my stories.

Part I

Guangzhou

Chapter One

Not Enough Nail Polish

When I was five, my kindergarten instructor asked me to stop painting my nails. She explained that none of my classmates had access to nail polish, so I should try not to make them feel bad. I did not understand.

I lived in Guangzhou, one of the liveliest cities in China. My two-bedroom, fourth-floor apartment sat on the edge of the city's hustle and bustle. From my windows, I could look onto a major boulevard that hummed and screeched with automobiles, bicycles, and pedestrians. Railroad tracks snaked around the outer edges of the boulevard and marked an unofficial edge to the city center. Trains sped along the tracks at all hours, blaring loud sirens and blinking bright lights, often rousing my entire neighborhood from our slumber in the depth of the night.

My parents, my brother, and I shared one of the bedrooms in our apartment, while my paternal grand-parents and an uncle shared the other. Another uncle worked in a nearby city and returned home sporadically, sometimes once a week, sometimes once a month. When he returned, he slept in the living room. We shared the kitchen and the bathroom with the family next door.

If our unit was cramped, I did not notice. Across the hall, a couple close to my parents' age and their two children all shared a room that was no larger than my living room. Next door, an elderly woman and her two adult daughters lived in one room. The elderly woman's husband worked in a nearby city and visited on weekends. When he retired, he, too, came to live with his family in their one-room unit next door. The couple's son was undergoing "reeducation through labor" somewhere for having committed petty crimes during his youth. As the years passed, he would be released and would return to live in the same room as his family. My parents often reminded me that I was fortunate to live in such a big, comfortable unit. Not everyone in Guangzhou had so much space. We did in part because we were lucky: the government bureaucrats who were responsible for doling out housing units looked favorably upon my father's completion of a four-year stint as soldier in the People's Liberation Army.

Our apartment did not come with running hot water or modern toilet facilities. I did not complain or aspire to anything better because in the late 1970s and early 1980s, the rest of Guangzhou did not have such amenities either. Nearly everyone in my city and country boiled water for drinking, cooking, and showering. Like others in my family, I took my showers in the kitchen because it was more spacious than the bath-

room. Each time, I used a giant plastic cup to bail water from a bucket. Usually, the bucket consisted of a
pot of boiling hot water mixed with cold water from
the tap. I never asked why we did not boil more than
one pot of hot water for showering. Maybe one bucket
was what most other people in Guangzhou used.
Maybe my family did not wish to waste water, every
drop of which cost money. Maybe we were trying not
to waste the coal that fired the stove. Each time we
purchased more of it, we had to make multiple trips to
carry the black cylindrical blocks up four flights of
stairs before stacking them in our kitchen. All I knew
was that once winter began, I eagerly waited for the
weather to get colder. When it became cold enough,
my parents did away with the requirement that their
children shower every day, and then only once every
two or three nights did I need to stand in the kitchen,
defending myself against the cold with a bucket of
water and a plastic cup.

Our bathroom contained a squat toilet in front of a
gigantic ceramic tank from which we bailed water to
manually flush the waste away. It was a small, dark
room. Against one of the walls was a light bulb that
we turned on by pulling a string next to the door outside. When blackouts hit our neighborhood once a
week, once a month, or once every few months, I
would light a candle when I entered the bathroom and
watch the candle flicker. In the dark, faint rays of
light—and presumably some fresh air—flowed
through the small window high up near the ceiling.

Often, people emerged from the bathroom a little
bowlegged, trying to shake off the cramps and dis-

comfort of crouching. The husband of the elderly woman next door carried a small plastic stool with him into the bathroom if he needed to crouch. He was old and overweight and the stool allowed him to rest when the crouching became too unbearable.

My brother and I did not like the old man. He never smiled and when he coughed, it was so loud that it always scared me a little. Whenever he was around, my brother's penchant for mischief always kicked into high gear. One day, my brother convinced me to wait with him for the old man to walk into the bathroom with his plastic stool. We then quickly ran to the bathroom door and yanked on the string outside. As the light went off, we heard the old man grunt in the pitch darkness. My brother and I quickly ran away and laughed until we keeled over. I felt a little guilty afterwards but I always followed my brother, who was four years older and infinitely wiser. We repeated our prank a few times. It must have been obvious to the old man that we were the culprits, but he never once complained to my parents. He rarely spoke to anyone in my family and despite our mischief, he did not seem inclined to start. After the second or third time we pulled our prank, my mother found her children giggling uncontrollably in the bedroom. She extracted a confession out of us and forbade us to ever engage in the prank again. Afterwards, my brother insisted that we should continue when Mother was not looking but I refused. I always listened to my parents, no matter how wise my brother was. He called me a chicken but must have disliked the idea of turning off the bathroom light and then running somewhere to laugh by himself. So he, too, left the old man alone.

My brother and I never dared to pull the same prank on our grandfather. He was older than the man next door but he was slim and more agile. When my brother misbehaved, which was quite often, Grandpa beat him. He never beat me, though. I rarely misbehaved. When I did, it was almost always at the urging of my brother, who normally ended up being the one whom Grandpa punished. Besides, I was Grandpa's first little girl. He had had six sons and one grandson before I came along. He was ready for a girl when I arrived, and he doted on me. His doting was not warm and fuzzy because Grandpa was not a warm and fuzzy man, but everyone knew that I was his favorite.

Grandpa had little to say to me, though, and being a shy and quiet girl, I usually had little to say to him. Maybe that was why he liked me. He was a man of few words and preferred to read, practice Tai-chi or take long walks. He did not like children or adults who talked incessantly. My brother talked incessantly.

My parents often reminded me that Grandpa was very well-educated and had gone to college. It was an honor for our family. His wife, his sons, his daughter-in-law, and most people in China did not have a university degree. When I asked why not, my parents answered that Grandpa had done better in school than many, many others and had done so before China's "liberation," before it became difficult to go to college and before the government and others began to perceive it as anti-revolutionary to have a good education. By liberation, my parents were referring to the founding of the People's Republic of China by the Chinese Communist Party in 1949, but I did not know who had liberated whom from what, nor did I ask why liberation had led to less education for everyone, not more. All I knew was that before he retired, Grandpa had been the chief civil engineer of a major company that blasted mountains for mining. Prior to that, he had spent many years constructing houses, bridges, tunnels, roads, and other engineering feats.

My mother often told her children that we should study as hard as Grandpa had done and go to college when we grew up. My brother always snickered a bit when Grandpa's name came up, perhaps because he secretly hated Grandpa for beating him. I did not mind aspiring to be just like Grandpa. I liked clinging onto him as his favorite.

Grandma was the only person who did not seem impressed with Grandpa's education. Though many of her female contemporaries could barely read and write, Grandma had graduated from the most prestigious all-girls junior high school in Guangzhou. Despite, or perhaps because of, her own impressive level of education, she often accused Grandpa of being an idiot who read many books but possessed little common sense. She told my brother and me of the time when Grandpa was thrown into detention during China's Cultural Revolution. He and a group of his colleagues were instructed at work to write slogans denouncing those whom Chairman Mao Zedong had labeled as traitors, renegades or "capitalist roaders." When a colleague arrived at work late, sat next to Grandpa and asked what needed to be done, Grandpa relayed the instructions. To make sure that his colleague understood, Grandpa gave an example: "Make sure you write 'Down with Liu Shaoqi,' not 'Down with Mao Zedong.'" Other colleagues overheard Grandpa's instructions and immediately accused him of thinking anti-revolutionary, anti-Mao Zedong thoughts. After all, if he was not thinking "Down with Mao Zedong," how could he have said it out loud and told someone else not to write it? They reported him to their superiors, who threw Grandpa into detention. Apparently, most work units had their own detention centers during the Cultural Revolution. Grandpa's unit did not abuse him, but they detained him for several days, publicly denounced him and made him formally confess his transgressions.

Only years later did I learn that Liu Shaoqi was a former President of China who had battled for power with the great Chairman Mao and lost. In the Cultural Revolution, he was widely considered a traitor, a renegade and a capitalist roader.

"Isn't he stupid?" Grandma laughed, "Who would walk around telling people not to write 'Down with Mao Zedong'? Nobody with a brain would have even uttered those words in the Cultural Revolution."

My brother laughed too and agreed. I felt horrible that Grandpa had been locked up, even if only for a few days. Meanwhile, I felt a little stupid myself—I had no idea what Grandpa had done wrong. I did not know what the Cultural Revolution was.

Whatever it was, I was relieved that it was no longer around to lock Grandpa up in detention. All the adults around me seemed relieved as well, though they often appeared uneasy when discussing it. Mother had noted more than once that had the Cultural Revolution not occurred, she and my father could have probably attended college as well. My father was no slouch; he was a senior mechanic for a fishing company and was regularly trailed by groups of apprentices who deferentially addressed him as "Master Ma." But he had not gone to college and could not become an engineer like Grandpa. His service in the military shielded him from much of the political chaos of the Cultural Revolution. No one dared to accuse a former soldier of being anti-revolutionary. Nevertheless, the military had prevented my father from finishing high school—he had been drafted in tenth grade upon passing a physical exam. For the next four years, he hated serving in the military because life was hard and there was often not enough to eat. In any case, the Cultural Revolution ended the year after I was born, when Chairman Mao passed away, and my parents often told me and my brother that we were fortunate not to have to grow up in it.

Being the fortunate child that I was, I attended a reputable kindergarten on the other side of my city five days a week, coming home only for the weekends. My brother attended an elementary school that was a fifteen-minute walk away from our apartment. When school was out during weekends, holidays, and winter and summer vacations, our parents always found fun things for their children to do. Each summer, they took us swimming. On weekends, they often took us to the park. Usually, we visited the park down the street from our apartment, where we hiked, row-boated, and walked around the lake. Sometimes, my parents took us to Children's Park, where we played on swings, seesaws, and slides. There weren't any roller coasters or water slides, but we did not know what those were anyway.

Sometimes, my parents took us to the zoo, where my brother and I marveled at the different animals and eagerly waited for the peacocks to show off their plumage. Each time, children lined up outside of the peacocks' cage to scream: "Peacocks are not as pretty as ravens! Peacocks are not as pretty as ravens!" My brother informed me that hectoring was the best way to get the peacocks to show off their plumage—they would want to prove that they were in fact prettier than the ravens. My brother always screamed the loudest. I usually stood next to him quietly because I did not really know what ravens were and I felt uncomfortable saying that they were prettier than the peacocks. If the peacocks did not do as we wished, my brother always blamed me for not screaming. My father would laugh, and my most fervent wish for the rest of the day would be to scream with my brother at the peacocks on our next visit to the zoo.

———

In the middle of my idyllic life in Guangzhou, when I was three or four, relatives I had never seen began trickling in from Hong Kong, a nearby city that was a British colony. These relatives were better-dressed and more urbane than anyone we knew in China. The women always wore heels and makeup, neither of which my mother or the adult women I knew owned.

The men walked with a certain swagger, as if they were better than the men in China. In some ways, we all believed that these visitors were better than all of us. Each time, they showed up bearing gifts, such as toys not available in China, clothes more fashionable than what we wore, and electronic devices that we had never owned or seen. Just as often, they took us to dinner at fancy restaurants that we could not afford.

More and more white tourists from America and other Western countries were showing up in Guangzhou as well. My relatives visited more and more frequently and brought me more and more gifts. I was too young to know that my city was special. In 1979, China normalized relations with the United States. Under our new leader Comrade Deng Xiaoping, Guangzhou and nearby cities such as Shenzhen became the first Chinese cities to welcome foreign investment in the country's effort to open up to the world.

One day, a Hong Kong relative whom I had never previously met presented me with two bottles of nail polish, one red and one pink. No one I knew owned or used nail polish. I assumed that it was something cool. Everything that my relatives brought in from Hong Kong was by definition cool.

Upon seeing the nail polish, I held it in my hands and looked perplexed.

"Ma Ying[1] doesn't know what to do with her gift." The woman who had presented me with the gift laughed. Everyone else visiting from Hong Kong

---

[1] In Chinese, the last name comes before the first name.

laughed as well. I looked even more perplexed.

"Don't worry, Ma Ying, I'll show you." The woman opened the bottle of red nail polish, grabbed my hand and proceeded to paint my nails. Afterwards, she smiled and told me not to let my fingers touch anything for at least ten minutes so as to prevent the nail polish from smearing. I looked at my outstretched fingers.

"Do you like it?" she asked.

"Yes," I shyly replied. I still had no idea who she was, but it did not matter. For the first time in my life, my nails were red.

The weekend passed. Our relatives left and returned to Hong Kong. On Monday morning, I returned to kindergarten. This was my first week at school with painted nails.

Mother instructed me not to tell instructors and classmates that we had relatives who regularly visited from Hong Kong. She did not explain, and I would not have understood, that she did not wish to risk being condemned as a "capitalist roader" should that label become fashionable again. After all, it was not long ago that China condemned, often violently, anyone's connection to a capitalist society. Mother instructed me to say that I did not know anything if others asked about my new nail polish or anything else that I had received from Hong Kong.

On Monday, I forgot about Mother's warnings as soon as I walked through the door of my classroom in kindergarten. Waving my hands around, I showed off my nails. Everybody came to look. Then they began to bombard me with questions. With a fair amount of glee, I answered as quickly as possible.

"What is this?"

"Nail polish."

"What's nail polish?"

"You paint color onto your nails and then let it dry."

"Where does it come from?"

"My relatives brought it for me from Hong Kong."

"Who are your relatives?

"They are people who buy me cool stuff."

"I want my nails painted too."

"You would need nail polish."

"Where do I get it from? Can my parents buy it at the store?"

"I don't think so. You can't buy it at stores in China."

"Why not?"

"Because they don't have them."

"Do you have any more nail polish?"

"Yes, but it's at home."

Teacher Lee, our instructor, soon joined the ruckus.

"Let me see," she said. "Wow, Ma Ying, your nails look so pretty."

I smiled, happy to receive the compliment. More and more children swarmed around me, curious and envious.

The boys in my class wanted nail polish too. No one had told us that nail polish was for women. We all just instinctively wanted products that China did not have and that the wealthier, developed world could offer. When I started to paint my nails, everyone else—

boys and girls alike—wanted to do the same. My access to the outside world, perhaps more so than the nail polish, provided me with unprecedented bragging rights.

As the week progressed, my nail polish began to chip and peel. So I started to dole out the chipped and peeled pieces to the class as if I were a pedestrian handing out change to beggars. I gave the biggest pieces to my friends. I tantalized classmates I did not like by suggesting that I would give them nail polish chips if they asked nicely. When they did, I inevitably told them that they had not asked nicely enough. For the classmates I really, really liked (mainly a few of the boys in the class), I went as far as to slowly peel away my nail polish before they cracked or chipped, producing small, flat red sheets that were prettier than the oddly shaped chunks that broke off.

My system did not provide for everyone. Those unlucky ones who did not benefit from my handouts walked away empty handed. Those blessed with my favoritism walked away with peels or chips of dried nail polish to carry in their pockets, but no color on their nails.

Finally, in the middle of our kindergarten's—and our country's—nail polish scarcity, the children of my class found a solution: they started to paint their nails with colored pencils. We did not use crayons because we did not know that crayons existed. We knew for sure, though, that no one besides me had nail polish. With colored pencils, my classmates at least had a substitute. When used, this inferior substitute left sloppy marks and scratches on my classmates' fingernails. Even those students with good coloring skills could only successfully cover the nails on one hand, as everyone found it difficult to color with his or her less adroit hand. Moreover, the pigments in our colored pencils washed off easily. As such, my classmates had to recolor repeatedly each day. Soon enough, my classmates spent less and less time running around the playground and more and more time coloring their nails.

They continued to beg me for more nail polish chips or peels at every opportunity. By the end of the week, I was running out of handouts. So I told my friends, "When I go home this weekend, I will paint my nails again and can give you more nail polish next week." My friends nodded eagerly.

Except for one girl. She said dismissively, "We won't need her next week."

We all asked, "Why not?"

"Because we can ask our parents to buy nail polish for us over the weekend."

"You won't be able to find any," I corrected her.

"My parents will know where to get it," she insisted.

I shrugged, not liking the prospect that a resourceful parent might take away my bragging rights. However, I was convinced that no one else in my class had relatives who visited from Hong Kong.

That weekend, I went home and painted my nails pink. When I showed them to my mother, she looked a bit concerned. "Maybe you shouldn't play around with nail polish this young," she said. "You are just a kid. We don't want you to become vain."

I was definitely too young to understand the word "vain." Mother, an elementary schoolteacher, tried to explain: Children were too young to wear makeup or fancy clothing; they were just supposed to be children; obsessing about looks at such a young age was not good. She spared me the Communist teachings that she regularly imparted to her students, which instructed that only inner beauty and devotion to our great country and the Chinese Communist Party mattered. Regardless, I was not listening. Whatever Mother was saying, I knew that when I wore nail polish, I was prettier and more special than all the other kindergarteners in my class.

"Noooooooooooo, I really like it!" I protested.

Mother could tell that her message was not getting through. So she gave up. She could have, but did not, confiscate my nail polish. Maybe it was because I had not committed an offense after all, and maybe secretly, she agreed that the nail polish looked nice on me.

The next Monday, I returned to kindergarten, ready to show off my nail polish again. The girl who had threatened to get nail polish from her parents had returned with her nails unpainted. The other children had returned eager to ask me for more handouts before coloring their nails with colored pencils again.

The parents of my class, however, had something different in mind. As they dropped off their children, many stopped to have a word with Teacher Lee. Like my mother, they looked concerned. As they chatted, Teacher Lee nodded and glanced at me several times.

Later that day, Teacher Lee took me aside.

"Will you stop painting your nails, for the good of

the class?" she asked with the utmost sincerity.

I did not understand.

"But why?"

"Because none of the other children have nail polish," Teacher Lee quietly explained. "Over the weekend, many of them asked their parents to buy it for them, but as you know, nail polish is not widely available in Guangzhou. Look at your classmates. They spend their time ruining their nails with colored pencils. They all feel bad that they don't have nails like yours."

I listened to Teacher Lee in silence, not really feeling bad for my classmates but definitely feeling bad about the prospect of having to give up painting my nails.

Sensing my hesitation, Teacher Lee tried a different approach. "Your classmates are also making a mess with the colored pencils. They throw them all over the floor and the playground and the other instructors and I have to clean up afterwards. I know you are a good kid. You have always listened to what we teach you. So I know that you'll help the instructors keep the classroom clean. After this week, will you stop painting your nails?"

Usually, my instructors did not make such requests. They would just tell us what we needed to do. If we did not do as instructed, we were either punished or our parents were advised to punish us.

Something was different this time. I could not tell what it was. Teacher Lee was no longer exuding the confidence and optimism that she exuded when she told us, as she regularly did, that we were the flowers of our country, or when she encouraged us to be kind, generous, and honest.

Had I been older, she probably would have explained that China's economy did not offer the plethora of goods that the outside world, like Hong Kong or the United States, did. Perhaps she would have shared that she had never painted her nails, either. Perhaps I would have asked why China was so impoverished and why it did not have what citizens of other societies took for granted. Perhaps I would have understood what she did not explain: our country had emerged only a few years before from our decade-long Cultural Revolution, in which millions perished or were ruined in the midst of political struggles and campaigns, and we had bidden farewell less than a decade before that to the Great Leap Forward, in which millions starved to death following government edicts for production and collectivization. Had I been older, perhaps I would have understood why there was not enough nail polish for everybody.

But I was not older. It was not my fault that Guangzhou or China was poor. My instructor, out of concern for the other children of her class, had decided to ask me to share the burden of our country's economic backwardness. After all, in the brave new world of China's reform and opening up to the outside world, we were now discovering together just how much we did not have.

Teacher Lee was asking me for a favor, one that I did not have to grant. Yet she somehow appeared to have faith that I would grant it.

Feeling pretty was a very new thing for me. Being

a good kid, on the other hand, was something for which I had striven for as long as I could remember. Despite everything that I was too young to understand, I knew that the last thing that I wanted was to refuse to listen to or heed the words of my elders. I slowly nodded my head, still not totally convinced that I was actually going to give up painting my nails.

Regardless, Teacher Lee looked relieved. She said before walking away, "You are a very good kid, Ma Ying. I always knew you were."

Later that day, Teacher Lee informed our class that she would be confiscating everyone's colored pencils. We had been making far too much of a mess, she told us. She would reissue the colored pencils when she believed that we could behave better. She did not mention my name. My classmates grumbled but turned in their colored pencils.

The next day, I stopped doling out nail polish chips and returned to playing with my friends. On the playground, Fei stood at the far end by himself, with his back turned toward everyone. He was one of the rowdiest children in my class. Normally, he chased others, got into fights, and created a ruckus. He was also the boy who made the playground safe for me. If another kindergartener were to hit me or tease me, he would often come to my defense, even if he was sometimes impatient that defending me took him away from his own games.

During the previous week, I had peeled off a large piece of nail polish for Fei, but since then I had been too busy to pay attention to him. I walked to where he was on the playground. As I approached, I realized what he was doing: he was still coloring his nails! He must have hidden a small colored pencil in his pocket. He was now using it in a corner of the playground, hoping that Teacher Lee would not notice.

"Fei, come play with us," I said as I walked up behind him. He did not turn around. I looked at his nails. He drew on them hard and I could see the sharp pink lines on each nail. He kept drawing, trying to color in the areas in between the sharp lines and his cuticles.

"Stop coloring, Teacher Lee says you can ruin your nails like that. Come play with me."

"I won't be playing today," Fei mumbled. He did not turn his head.

"But you always play."

Fei did not respond.

I peeled off a big piece of pink nail polish from one of my fingernails and put it under his nose. "You don't have to color your nails. Here, I'll give you the polish from my nails. I can even give you all of it if you want. I won't give it to anyone else."

He shook his head.

"C'mon, take it," I grabbed his arm. This time, he barely shook his head.

I tried one last time. "If you won't take my nail polish, then I'm not going to play with you anymore."

He did not respond, and did not take my handout, so I let go of his arm and walked away. Back in the center of the playground, I watched him standing in the same corner, with his back turned toward everyone. He was not supposed to be coloring his nails in the first place. My parents informed me over the weekend that nail polish was not made for boys.

Somehow, knowing that did not make me feel better.

Maybe it was the image of Fei with his head buried in his nails; maybe it was the quiet hope for understanding in Teacher Lee's voice when she asked me for a favor; maybe it was all that I could not yet understand about China as it reopened its doors to the world. I stopped painting my nails. The next weekend, my mother did not have to explain to me again why it was bad for a little girl to become vain. When she asked me why I did not want to paint my nails, I told her I no longer felt like it.

In due time, all of my nail polish peeled off, and the color marks on my classmates' nails faded away. Teacher Lee was right. Once I stopped painting my nails, the other children forgot about painting theirs. She ultimately reissued colored pencils to us.

Fei returned to the playground and once again took up the task of being my protector. Before the end of the school year, he crowned himself as the emperor of our class and announced me as his empress.

When I returned home the following weekend, the trains continued to roar at night and wake me from my slumber. Grandpa continued to favor me over my brother. My brother continued his mischief-making. My parents continued to run around trying to make their children's lives more comfortable. China still did not have nail polish, but I was now an empress, and I did not look back.

Chapter Two

My Brother's Little Tail

The kindergarten years flew by and soon it was time for elementary school. So I left the reputable kindergarten across town for a respectable elementary school close to home.

My new school was only a fifteen-minute walk from my apartment. It was the best school in my neighborhood and a top-notch school in my city. The school did not accept just anybody—I had to take a test to get in.

Once I got in, instead of spending the week away at kindergarten, I got to spend every day at home. I could no longer be Fei's empress. Indeed, I had no idea where Fei went after kindergarten. In exchange, I got to see my family more often. In particular, I now had oodles and oodles of "face time" with my brother.

I followed him everywhere, even though he terrorized me at every opportunity. He took my toys, made fun of me, threatened to beat me and often did. Being four years older and quite a bit heavier, he always won our fistfights. Punching him never seemed to hurt him sufficiently, so I resorted to cutting him with my nails. He never liked the scrapes that I inflicted or the faint traces of blood that flowed from the wounds. He dominated our physical scuffles, though, and I always hated him when he won. Nonetheless, I forgave him after every scuffle and continued to follow him around, convinced that he knew much more about the world than I.

Before I entered elementary school, my brother's favorite instrument of fear was our family's little black dog. It was, for all intents and purposes, his dog. It barked fiercely and always looked as if it were ready to bite. My brother took the dog with him everywhere he went, encouraging it to bark at and chase after the little girls in the neighborhood and his own sister. Little girls would run away and cry when my brother sent the dog after them. My brother would laugh.

Thankfully, the dog did not get to terrorize me throughout my childhood. One day, my family ate it. Owning dogs as pets was considered bourgeois and was banned by the city of Guangzhou. Eating dog meat, however, was perfectly legal. Every winter, the city's residents made a habit of purchasing dog meat to make stew. In the cold and without any heat, the dog meat kept us warm. Temporary ownership of a dog before it was killed and eaten was tolerated, too, as long as no one reported the enjoyment of this bourgeois pastime to our neighborhood committee, which consisted of unelected resident representatives who settled disputes, enforced government edicts, scrutinized public and private behavior, and denounced any offense against the state. So my family got rid my brother's little black dog before anyone filed a complaint against us.

The day our dog was killed was a festive day. My family invited a few friends and relatives to join us for stew. My brother refused to eat the dog meat and cried for days, accusing the adults of killing his friend. All the adults laughed, teasing him for being so silly. I laughed too because I had always hated the dog and had hated my brother each time he used it to terrorize me.

Without his dog, my brother just found other ways to engage in mischief. He continued to dislike our grandfather and did all he could to pull pranks on him. Whenever possible, my brother tried to convince me to join him. As he explained it, he would let me join the fun if I bore the blame. Because I was Grandpa's favorite, Grandpa would never punish me. I usually agreed. Though I liked Grandpa a lot more than my brother did, I could rarely resist the excitement my brother's pranks offered. As far as I was concerned, even if I admitted that I had devised the pranks, Grandpa would never believe me and would punish my brother anyway.

The summer after I graduated from kindergarten, my brother and I attempted to execute one of his pranks on multiple hot afternoons. Because Grandpa's mouth often fell open when he slept, my brother decided that we should roll up small paper balls to throw into his mouth when he took afternoon naps in the living room.

I giggled at the thought, and giggled even more at

the sight of it. On our first try, we could not succeed, probably because we were too excited and too busy laughing. So we tried again, and again. When my brother finally managed to throw a rolled-up paper ball into Grandpa's mouth, Grandpa let out a loud noise and started to cough. My brother and I quickly ran away, afraid that Grandpa would wake up to beat us. He did not, but our father, who witnessed the prank and the giggling, became concerned that his father might choke on the paper balls. So even though he, too, laughed at our prank, he forbade us from ever engaging in it again.

I could not be sure if Grandpa ever learned of our prank. If he did, he never became angry with me. I was still his favorite, and he often took me to places without my brother. One day, Grandpa sat in a big wooden chair under the window in our living room reading his newspapers and magazines. I stood before his chair and asked him to play with me. Grandpa never played with his grandchildren. This time was going to be no different. He shook his head at my request and tried to concentrate on his reading.

"Grandpa, will you take me to the park?"

"Hmm?" Grandpa let out a noise, still trying to read.

"Grandpa, take me to Children's Park, please?"

"Children's Park?"

"Yes, it's not that far away and we'll be back before dinner."

Much to my surprise, Grandpa put down his reading materials. Rarely did he interrupt his reading for anything.

Then he got up from the chair. I still was not sure that he had agreed.

"So we'll go?"

"Yes."

"Yaaaaaaaay!!!!" I grabbed Grandpa's hand and off to the park we went.

I knew that my brother would be jealous when he found out, and the thought of it gave me great joy. But what if we ran into him on his way home? Would we then be obligated to take him with us? I was not sure. So I told Grandpa to hurry.

"C'mon, Grandpa, the park is going to close soon." It was early in the afternoon, and I knew better than anyone else that the park would stay open for at least a few more hours.

Grandpa did not argue with me but also did not pick up his pace. Thankfully, we managed to make it down four flights of stairs and out of our neighborhood without running into my brother.

When we arrived at the park, I was so excited that I ran around from my favorite slides to my favorite swings. Then I noticed that something was different. In past visits to the park, I could always go and find my brother. Even if we started in different parts of the playground, we could always play together, especially if I nagged him enough or if he felt the need to show off something new that he had just learned. But my brother was not there that day, and Grandpa was too old to play with me. So I roamed the playground by myself. After about half an hour, I was relieved when Grandpa came to take me home.

Back in our apartment complex, a few steps from

our building, Grandpa and I ran into my brother.

"Where did you just come from?" he demanded to know.

"Grandpa took me to Children's Park," I bragged.

"Why did he take you without taking me?"

"Well, you weren't there when we left."

"That's no fair!"

I laughed. This was the moment I had been waiting for.

Though he was an integral part of our conversation, Grandpa seemed oblivious to it. He usually had little to say to my brother. On this day, it was no different—he simply continued walking. My parents returned home later in the afternoon, and upon hearing my brother's complaint, they laughed too. Mother observed that Grandpa had taken me to the park because I was a good girl. He would have never taken my brother anywhere alone because my brother was a troublemaker. I felt special that Grandpa liked me more, but I never went to Children's Park again without my brother.

———

Though Grandpa favored me over my brother, I knew that my brother was many times smarter than I. Everyone in my family and all the adults we encountered told me so.

He was a fifth grader when I began attending his elementary school. For months before the school accepted me, Mother worried that I would fail my entrance exam. She told all our friends and family that she had not worried at all when my brother had taken his exam four years before. Whenever he opened his mouth, adults always marveled at how smart, clever, and adorable he was. By contrast, I was often scared of strangers or too shy to say much in their presence. When adults I did not know asked me questions, I did not like to respond, and preferred to cling onto an adult whom I did know, like my parents or grandparents.

Normally, my shyness was not a problem. It helped make me the quiet and good girl who always stayed out of trouble and listened to her elders. But in an oral exam in which a child's intelligence was discerned through questioning, my mother worried that my reticence would be interpreted as slowness or stupidity.

Her concern was warranted, because I nearly failed my entrance exam. What saved me was not that I overcame my shyness but that I was lucky. My interviewer turned out to be the school's music teacher. Though I mumbled in response to all her questions and clearly did not impress her with my intelligence, she discovered that I enjoyed singing in kindergarten and convinced me to sing for her. When I did, I danced for her too. My interviewer's eyes sparkled, and Mother knew that my song and dance had just gotten me into the school she wanted for me.

I did not really care much about getting into elementary school. The whole experience only further convinced me that my brother was leaps and bounds smarter than I. His interviewer at the oral exam, Mother told me, had fawned all over him from beginning to end. My interviewer, on the other hand, had been ready to reject me before I started singing.

None of that made me feel bad. I happily acknowledged my brother's superior knowledge and intelligence. When our relatives brought toys for us from Hong Kong, he was always the one who figured out how they worked. When adults had adult conversations, he always chimed in because he voraciously read newspapers and seemed to always know what was happening in our city and beyond. Whenever we played games, whether new or old ones, he always won. When new hotspots, trends, or entertainment options popped up in Guangzhou, my brother always knew before I did and always interpreted for me what everything meant and how we could enjoy them.

Playing with him, however, was not always painless. Even when he did not inflict pain purposely, he often did so accidentally. One Sunday, our parents took us to the neighborhood park. A new children's play area had just opened there, and a giant trampoline had been installed. The equipment was so new that few others in the city seemed to know about it. The park also charged extra for children to play in the new play area.

Always willing to keep their children happy, my parents forked over the extra admission fee. Excitedly, my brother and I ran up to the trampoline. It was large enough to accommodate at least fifty children, but my brother and I were the only ones there. It was our first trampoline. We had never seen one before. At first, I stood at the edge, wondering what to do. My brother jumped on first, and as he jumped up and down, I happily imitated him. As he jumped from one end of the trampoline to the other, I waved for him to join me where I was. He approached, hopping up and down, but as he took one big last hop and landed right next to me, my body shot up into the sky. When I landed on my behind, my knees jerked forward and knocked into my front teeth. Next thing I knew, blood was gushing out of my mouth.

Looking quite worried, my brother guided me off of the trampoline to find our parents. Seeing me bloody and in tears, their first question was: "What did he do to you?" I was too busy crying to answer. So my brother hurriedly answered for me: "I didn't do anything!"

When the bleeding from my mouth finally slowed, we discovered that one of my front teeth had been knocked loose. I explained what had happened but my parents decided that it was my brother's fault anyway. He was the older one; he should have known better and should have kept me safe.

"Don't play with him anymore," my father advised. "He doesn't know his strength and he'll just hurt you."

And hurt it did. Given that my tooth was loose, it hurt to eat for weeks afterwards. Finally, my father decided to put me out of my misery by yanking it out. But that created a fair amount of misery in and of itself. Most children in China did not visit the dentist for baby teeth removal. My father did what he had always done to remove my teeth: he tied a string around the loose tooth and yanked hard on it until the roots separated from the gums. It was a procedure that I always dreaded. In this case, I screamed and cried as blood gushed out of my mouth. Finally, after the tooth had been removed, my father laughed and reminded me again not to play with my brother in the future.

Soon enough, though, I forgot about my tooth and went back to following my brother everywhere. Even when I followed him under duress, I often became convinced afterwards that the experience had been worthwhile.

That was the case on the day my brother confiscated my bus money. Our parents had taken us out to lunch. They had to run errands afterwards. So they gave my brother one yuan and instructed him to take me home on the bus. Happily, almost too happily, my brother agreed.

With my parents out of sight, my brother started walking, and I followed behind. Within minutes, we stopped in front of a movie theater.

"What are we doing here?" I asked.

"We're not taking the bus home," my brother said. "We're going to see a movie and walk home afterwards."

"I don't want to walk home. It's really far."

"It'll take only thirty to forty minutes. Besides, I have the bus money. You can watch the movie with me, or you can walk home by yourself."

"But I don't know the way."

"Then you'll just have to wait for me to walk home with you."

"Mom and Dad told you to take me home!"

"Well, they're not here. Either you listen to me or you're not going home."

"But I don't want to walk."

"I don't care. You either watch the movie with me or you wait outside until I'm done."

Reluctantly, I went into the movie theater. My brother had decided that we would watch *Rambo II: First Blood* in English, with Chinese subtitles. This choice made my brother's offense still worse; I had never heard of the stupid film, and now I would have to watch it in a language I did not understand.

Very quickly, though, the movie made me forget that I did not speak English and that I had wanted to go home. *Rambo* offered all kinds of things I had never seen before: big explosions, hand-to-hand combat, shoot outs, nonstop violence, and a crazy hero who managed to subdue everyone else. It was my first American movie, my first foreign action flick, and it was incredible. Most Chinese movies I had seen up until then featured slogans praising China's socialist revolution and offered predictable plot lines condemning capitalists, anti-revolutionaries, or the Japanese. This movie was different, and for about two hours, I could not take my eyes off the screen.

When it was over, my brother bragged. "That was a great! Did you like it?" Reluctantly, I said that I did.

"I told you! I knew this would be a great movie."

"How did you know?"

"I just do, I know where all the cool stuff is. That's why you should always listen to me."

I did not say anything, but I silently agreed. I had never been so excited after seeing a movie. I was sure that few people I knew had ever seen such a movie. New and cool things from the outside world were surfacing every day in my life and in my city. I did not always know where, why, or how, but I always had my brother as my guide. He even told me that Rambo's name in real life was *see tai lone*. I had never heard of Sylvester Stallone, so this Cantonese rendition of the name was good enough for me.

During the long walk home, my brother instructed me not to tell our parents that we had gone to see a movie. I gladly agreed, having forgotten by then that my brother had coerced me into our movie outing. When my parents returned home later in the day, they did not suspect a thing.

A story in a children's magazine accurately summed up our sibling relationship. My brother read the story out loud the evening he found it. I had already gone to sleep, but Mother made the unusual decision of letting me climb out of bed to listen. Titled "My Little Tail," the story described a brother and sister who were about our ages. Just like me, the sister was four years younger than her brother and followed him around everywhere. She played with his toys, read his books, and bugged him nonstop. Sometimes, he became annoyed because he thought she was a pest. Sometimes, he forbade her from following him. She would get upset but would continue to follow and pester him. Like me, she always wanted to participate in her brother's activities. When he drew two diagrams for his art class, she colored them in his absence. When he returned and noticed the disastrous color schemes, he yelled at her for ruining his homework. She cried and told him she was simply trying to help. He felt horrible. Subsequently, he drew solid black circles over her colors, turning his diagrams into a giant panda. He had fixed his homework. When his little sister stopped crying, he concluded that she was his little tail and he was, for the most part, very happy about that.

When the reading ended, I exclaimed, "I'm my older brother's little tail!" My brother concurred. Mother laughed and then told me to hurry and go back to sleep.

———

Unfortunately, when my brother reached junior high and I entered third grade, I began to feel less and less like his little tail. All of a sudden, he grew much taller. We no longer attended the same school, and he found a whole new group of friends. He began to use new lingo and always told me I was stupid when I did not understand. He used more profanity and began mentioning names of people whom I did not know and had never met. Just as in elementary school, I wanted to join his conversations with his friends when they visited our home, but each time I was shooed away.

In the middle of all of this confusion, my math instructor, Teacher Fu, walked into class one day with a stack of booklets. After handing them out, she announced that our math class was not going to take place that day.

"You are all going to spend the hour confessing," she declared. Each student in the class was supposed to describe our—or someone else's—wrongdoing in his or her booklet.

"Now the school knows that each of you, or someone you know, has behaved wrongly," Teacher Fu continued. "Instead of punishing you, we're giving you this chance to come clean."

The students looked at each other. A couple of confused classmates raised their hands.

"What type of 'wrongdoing' are we supposed to confess?" one brave soul asked.

Teacher Fu seemed annoyed. She raised her voice and said sternly, "You all know what you've done wrong. So don't pretend you don't. If you try to lie, we will know. Any more questions?"

"But I don't understand," another student piped up.

"Don't play dumb," Teacher Fu scolded us. "You need to confess your wrongdoing. You've all done something wrong. Alternatively, you can write about someone else who has done something wrong. Now start writing."

The rest of the class no longer dared to ask more questions. In silence, we sheepishly began writing.

I wondered what the school knew about me. I believed Teacher Fu when she said that the school knew all about my wrongdoings—I always believed my teachers. Now I was genuinely worried. Did the school already know that I had relatives from Hong Kong who brought me toys and clothing from the world of the capitalist running dogs? Did it know that I really, really liked American movies, even though I had only seen one? Did it know the secret I had never told anyone: that my parents had applied for the whole family to immigrate to America?

Then I remembered all those occasions when I had told lies, had not shared my toys with friends, or had thrown things out the window of my fourth-floor apartment. The list went on and on. The more I thought about it, the more mortified I became. Ten minutes passed and I still had not written a word. Everyone else, though, appeared to be busy writing. Some of the other students had already completed multiple pages of their "confessions."

I was too afraid to report on my own behavior. It was scary to contemplate what the school might do to me. As the clock ticked I felt more and more desperate, so I opted to reveal someone else's wrongdoing.

"My brother," I began writing, "entered junior high school this year and has been hanging out with the wrong crowd. They all seem to be up to no good. He is not taking school as seriously as before and his new friends are a bad influence on him. They swear constantly. Quite likely, they skip school sometimes. Maybe they smoke, too. I think my brother is very wrong to let himself be influenced by these people. He may be on the edge of the law. I condemn his behavior and his associations."

I had no evidence that my brother was doing anything wrong; in fact, I had no idea at all what he was doing. I merely knew less about his life in junior high school than I did about his life in elementary school, and his current friends appeared to be more intimidating than his former friends. Regardless, the truth did not matter. I did not want the school to come after me for my wrongdoings. So I gave my brother away, spurred on by the threatening tone of Teacher Fu's voice and my blank little booklet. At the end of class, I turned in a confession that combined suspicion with fantasy and incoherence with fear.

When class ended, Teacher Fu collected our booklets. Before she sent us home, she sternly informed us, "We will read your confessions. If any of you made anything up, we will know."

The students walked out of the classroom, all of us looking a bit dejected after the day's classroom exercise.

On the way home, I began to worry about what could happen to my brother as a result of my confession.

"Hey, what did you confess about?" Lan asked. She and I walked home together nearly every day. Often, we were joined by a few other classmates. That day, it was just the two of us.

Deeply troubled by my own confession, I said, "I don't know. It didn't make any sense. I wrote something about my brother. What about you?"

"I confessed that I read 'yellow' novels and magazines."

"Really? When?"

"From time to time," Lan laughed, not appearing at all embarrassed. She was not a bad student but she was not particularly stellar either. Our teachers, however, liked her because she was always well-behaved. Her interests, as far as the rest of the class could tell, were sewing, knitting, cooking, and other activities related to the home. I had no idea that she even enjoyed reading, let alone reading risqué novels and magazines.

"Where do you get these novels and magazines from?" I asked.

"Sometimes I find them lying around at home when the adults are done reading."

"Do they know that you're reading them?

"I don't know. Probably not."

"Are you now going to stop reading them?"

"I said I was going to try my best," she smiled, looking rather sincere.

I did not smile back and started to feel stupid. Why had I not confessed to something like that? No one would have punished me or my brother for such a confession. At worst, they would have stopped me from reading dirty novels and magazines, which likely would not have been all that dirty to begin with.

What was going to happen to my brother now? Would someone take him away to prison on the basis of what I had revealed? For days after my confession, I lived in abject horror. I thought about warning my brother, but I did not because I knew that he would have certainly beaten me. So I remained silent, and my horror intensified.

Little did I know that mandatory confessions were a typical Communist requirement. Self-condemnation and condemnation of others were common methods our government employed to gather information and reinforce the state's authority.

Thankfully, nothing happened. Perhaps my statement had not been incriminating enough. No one came to take my brother away, and after a few weeks, I forgot about my confession. Over time, I got more used to his new life in junior high school and became more familiar with his new friends, and I went back to being his little tail, at least when he did not shoo me away. As we continued to explore Guangzhou and all the Western items that were surfacing in our city, he never found out that his little tail had earnestly betrayed him to China's state apparatus.

Chapter Three

The Gang Leader

"How could you?! You're the captain of the class. You are supposed to set an example for everyone else!"

My favorite instructor, Teacher Wang, was chastising me in front of my entire third-grade class. More furious than I had ever seen her, she pointed at me and at a boy standing alone in the front of the classroom, and thundered, "Stand up and explain yourself! Were you or were you not part of his gang?"

I looked at the boy standing in front of the classroom. It was the fall and the beginning of the school year. Our normally stuffy classroom seemed stuffier than usual. It was next to the little boys' room. When the wind blew in a certain direction, we all had to cover our noses. That day, there was no wind, no stench. All I could feel was my cheeks—they were red hot.

A gang was a danger to society. I was a model student who had been handpicked by my instructors to be the captain of my class since first grade. My position required no leadership skills, but I had the best

grades, a spotless record, and my instructors' favoritism. I had no business joining a gang, but I was indeed
a member of *his* gang.

His gang consisted of about half of the boys of our
class. From time to time, they practiced kung fu on a
rooftop in their neighborhood. They had no instructor
and no idea what they were doing, but they were un-
deterred. Like numerous other Chinese boys, they
dreamed of becoming like the mythical kung fu fig-
ures described in popular, and riveting, Chinese martial arts tales.

The summer before third grade, a female classmate who did not live in my neighborhood and had
never previously been to my home appeared at my
door with an invitation. Somewhat out of breath after
running up four flights of stairs, she declared that various boys in our class would like me to join their martial arts group.

"Everyone is already at practice. Can you come
with me now?" She asked.

"Yes." I did not even blink. She may have been the
one who just ran up four flights of stairs, but I was the
one trying to suppress my breathlessness.

I did not know, and did not ask, why the boys had
invited me to join their martial arts group. I assumed it
was because every Chinese martial arts story had a
heroine, and I accepted the invitation believing that
their story could have no better heroine than me.

I was, after all, the captain of the class. I proudly
occupied my position and dutifully carried out its
tasks. Each day, I stood in the front of the classroom
and called various classes to order. My position made

me less shy and less quiet. Though I was not mean, I often reprimanded my fellow students when they misbehaved. Just as often, I snitched on everyone, ranging from classmates who cheated on exams to those who got into fist-fights to those who dozed off during class. I was not just a model of studiousness; I was the assistant class disciplinarian.

My school delighted in my rule-abiding eagerness. Its system was designed to reward people like me. My captain's badge bore two solid horizontal bars, the maximum number allowed for captains between the first and fourth grades. Only two students in each class had the honor of wearing such a badge: the captain and her deputy. Below them, five students served as mini-captains and "led" smaller subsections of the class. Their badges bore only one bar. A few fifth and sixth graders served as super-captains of students from more than one class. Super-captains were all former captains who had demonstrated extraordinary competence. Their badges bore three solid bars.

These leadership positions rewarded good behavior, encouraged peer scrutiny of the lazy and the disobedient, created eyes and ears for the instructors, and inculcated leadership skills that conformed to the teachings dictated by the school and the government. In this system, I earnestly followed my instructors' teachings. They in turn appointed me to one leadership position after another. I was destined for super-captainship.

For now, in the third grade, I was the girl to envy. My friends wanted my grades, my title, and the fondness I elicited from our instructors. Those who were not my friends would want to be, or so I believed.

Yet some of my classmates seemed unimpressed. They were the boys who did not get good grades and did not care. They regularly got into scuffles in the schoolyard or otherwise disobeyed our teachers' orders. When reprimanded, they often appeared unfazed. Usually, they went about their trouble-making individually or in disparate small groups. From time to time, they resented my snitching, but more often than not, they appeared uninterested in all the qualities that made me worthy of admiration.

Now these boys had invited me to join their martial arts group. Nothing like it existed at our school, or anywhere else that I knew of, but I needed no explanation. All of us children, and many adults, were discovering the world of martial arts make-believe as it trickled in from Hong Kong, Taiwan, and elsewhere. It was an ancient world in which ordinary men and women became extraordinary by acquiring out-of-this-world kung fu skills and using those skills to seek truth, justice, love, or political order.

Two years before, numerous Chinese citizens, the children of my class included, got to watch *Shaolin Temple*, the first martial arts movie produced with foreign investment in modern China. Mesmerized, we entered a world of beautiful scenery, the inner sanctum of China's most famous Buddhist temple, a love story in which the hero chose duty over a girl, and spectacular sword fights and fist fights. For a while, every little boy in China wanted to be a martial arts hero, and every little girl wanted to play a part in the hero's adventures and conquests.

Around the same time, I started reading my first martial arts novel. I did not know then that its author was a Hong Kong-based novelist who was the most famous author of martial arts novels in the Chinese-speaking world. Back then, the Chinese government banned martial arts novels, which it believed contained the corrupt values of the capitalist West. My older brother, demonstrating once again that he was infinitely wiser than I, managed to obtain a copy of the novel from his network of friends. When he brought it home, he brought the world of martial arts to my fingertips.

For days, I sat motionless in the living room during every free moment, skipping over the words too complicated for a third grader to comprehend, devouring a story that took me to a fanciful world that appeared strange yet familiar, close yet so far away. The hero of the story, a peasant boy who stuttered, lost everything—including the love of his life and several of his fingers—in a battle with devious men, but ultimately acquired superb martial arts skills, sought revenge, and found a new love. Intuitively, I recognized the Chinese culture and history that gave life to martial arts tales and the logic that governed their code of honor. Hungrily, I grasped for everything in this world that modern China did not yet allow me to touch or see.

So when a group of boys in my class sent a messenger to fetch me for martial arts practice, I did not think twice. As soon as the message was conveyed, I ran down four flights of stairs with a girl I hardly knew to the rooftop of a neighborhood where I had never before set foot. The world that I had been reading about and watching on the movie screen could now be my own. It was as if someone had presented me with a dream that I had not yet dared to dream and promised to turn it into reality.

Nearly half of the boys in my class, including everyone who did not seem to care for my special status as captain, were on that rooftop. Never before had I seen them together in one place outside of class. They likely believed they could make their martial arts group great, perhaps as great as the famed Shaolin School. I was heartened that they had finally offered me their first indication of interest, their first sign of approval. Giddily, I believed in their vision of our shared future and its endless possibilities.

There was no mistaking who the leader of my new martial arts group was. He walked around the rooftop, sometimes instructing the other boys on their pseudo-martial arts and sometimes taking part. My invitation to join the group could not have been issued without his consent. In fact, it was likely issued based on his instructions.

He now stood alone in the front of the classroom because, unbeknownst to us third graders, our childhood fantasy had become an offense to the state. Despite my strict adherence to all that my instructors taught, I had crossed the line by joining a silly little martial arts group. On this afternoon in the fall of 1984, the boys and I discovered that we were also "gang members."

At the beginning of class, a student who was not a member of our group had snitched on us. Just as I thought it absurd to snitch on something so harmless, Teacher Wang exploded into a fit of rage. Her face was bright red. It was always red when she became angry with us.

Once she learned the identity of our pack's leader, she ordered him to stand in front of the classroom. She then bellowed, "Absolutely ridiculous! Is this what I have taught you? To form a gang?"

When a classmate informed her that the captain had participated in this "gang" activity as well, she pounded on the podium with her fist, her face now even redder. Teacher Wang was my favorite instructor. She was the last teacher I wanted to disappoint.

"Stand up and explain yourself! Were you or were you not part of his gang?" she demanded to know.

I slowly rose from my seat, mortified that I could be in real trouble for the first time in my life. Pounding on the podium with her fist, Teacher Wang went into a tirade for the next ten to fifteen minutes, condemning gang activity and those who chose its path.

Just as I began to think she had forgotten about me, she roared, "Were you or were you not part of his gang?"

There was no way to avoid answering and nowhere to escape. My cheeks were red hot, and I wondered if they were redder than Teacher Wang's face. Slowly, I made a noise that sounded like "N-o-o-o-o-o."

Teacher Wang apparently did not notice my hesitation or my bright red cheeks. She immediately unleashed her anger on the boy standing alone in the front of the class. "Was the captain part of your gang or not?"

I froze and waited for his response. He did not hesitate. "She was not," he said.

"And you spread rumors that she was! How dare you?!" Teacher Wang pounded her podium so loudly now that she looked as if she might reach over and hit him.

I could not fathom why watching or practicing pseudo-martial arts was gang activity, but as the captain of the class, I was not used to questioning my teachers' judgment and wanted even less for Teacher Wang to be angry with me. The boy, hardly a model student and no stranger to her disapproval, took on her anger, including that which he did not deserve.

"Who else was part of this illegal outfit?" Teacher Wang pounded on the podium again, her face even redder now. One by one, the boys from the rooftop stood up, as did the girl who served as their dutiful messenger. Unlike me, they did not abandon their friend or their "gang." As each one rose my face got redder and hotter.

For the next half hour, Teacher Wang continued pounding on the podium and instructed all the "gang members" to go home and reflect on their wrongdoing. From that day on, our martial arts group was disbanded.

I did not know then that the Chinese Communist state, to which we pledged our allegiance and sang songs expressing our devotion, was always, always suspicious of organized activity springing up outside its purview. It retained the ultimate power to condone or condemn civil society's spontaneity. As children, we just wanted to go outside and play. The rules of authoritarianism, however, applied to everyone from the aged to the innocent and were enforced by everyone from media censors to public security officials to guardians of the next generation, like Teacher Wang. Members of our "gang" could not fully understand what we had done wrong, but we admitted guilt and endured the reprimands, or in my case, denied involvement and let others take the blame.

Nothing serious or seriously harmful happened to us "gang members." After all, we were just children. We were not organizing on behalf of peasants rights, challenging the one-child policy, or rioting against Chinese control over ethnic border provinces such as Tibet or Xinjiang. Years later, those who did would discover at gun point or in prison the price their advocacy would exact. In 1984, I only knew that I had lied and that in turn, a boy had lied to protect me.

I did not even really know him. He never said much, but the other boys in the class always gravitated toward him. He never raised his hand in class and often did not turn in his homework on time. Every now and then he got into fights, but he seldom lost one. He never bullied anyone, as I often took it upon myself to interfere with or snitch on acts of bullying and I could not remember ever confronting him about his behavior. He regularly got into trouble but rarely behaved mischievously. Rather, our instructors seemed most incensed that he did not obey their orders and did not care for their approval.

Prior to that day on the rooftop, I could not remember if I had ever talked to him in the more than two years that we had been classmates. My closest friends lived near me or sat near me in class. He lived in a different part of the school's district, along with many others in his "gang." We walked to and returned from school on different routes. He also sat on the other side of the classroom. Even as members of the same martial arts group, we did not converse much.

Had I been curious about him before he stood alone in front of the classroom? I could not be sure. I tended to be curious about boys who were older and taller. This boy was not particularly tall or particularly good-looking. He was just another boy in my class. Now I owed him my position as captain of the class.

After the incident, I tried to ignore him. He said nothing, demanding from me neither the regret nor the gratitude to which I felt he was entitled. His friends followed suit and also said nothing.

My friends at first refused to let me off the hook. Ting, who often walked home with me and Lan, pestered me. "He saved you," she repeatedly said. "No, he didn't." I tried to stick to the official story that I had not been involved with his "gang." Ting did not fall for this. In front of Lan and a few others, she added, "Had it not been for him, you would have been in HUGE trouble." She smiled knowingly and even winked at Lan. Unlike Lan, Ting was an avid reader of all things serious. On our walks home, she liked to share with us the new knowledge she regularly gleaned from newspapers and magazines. Just weeks ago, as if revealing a great secret, she declared that the deadliest disease in the world was something called

AIDS. I did not believe her and insisted that heart attacks and lung cancer were far deadlier than whatever AIDS was.

Now, she seemed very pleased to share her knowledge of my guilt. Exasperated because she was right, I added to my lie. Smiling with as much nonchalance as I could muster, I responded, "I only went to their practices because I was curious about what they were doing; I did not actually join their group." Nobody present seemed convinced. Lan refrained from any pestering or condemnation. She never had a mean word for anybody. Perhaps she did not wish to start with me. I had no doubt, however, that she understood everything. Ting seemed content enough to know that my denial was a sham. Soon enough, she, too, fell silent.

I could not, however, stop thinking about my own guilt. Though Teacher Wang and the other instructors continued to shower me with praises and affection, I no longer looked upon my position as captain of the class with unreserved pride or enthusiasm. Some days, I was too disgusted with myself to wear my captain's badge to school.

Despite Teacher Wang's rage, I did not question the legitimacy of our martial arts group. Our school taught many of the essential principles that schools everywhere teach their children: respect your elders; love your parents; listen to your instructors; do your homework; work hard; do not steal; admit your mistakes and learn from them; be modest; and be generous to your classmates and friends. Deep down, I knew that our martial arts group had violated none of these tenets.

My offense, as it turned out, was against those teachings with Chinese characteristics: love China; love the Chinese people; believe in socialism; respect the great deeds carried out by Chairman Mao and his deputy Premier Zhou Enlai; remember the sacrifices China made to win World War II against the Japanese and the Civil War against the Kuomintang (the exiled regime in Taiwan); and follow the leadership of the Chinese Communist Party. These abstractions normally required no sacrifice and no concrete action from me, but they now stood between me and my fantasy world of martial arts. I may not have known why, but the authoritarian state I had been taught to love guarded its ability to sanction group activity jealously and if necessary, violently.

In the third grade, all I knew was that I hated my inability to stand with my "gang." Martial arts tales were riveting not only because the characters eviscerated their enemies in kung fu battles, but also because the good guys never betrayed their friends. In this world of fantasy, loyalty was just as important, if not more important, than the power of the fist or the sword. As the captain of the class and the model student up to whom all other classmates should look, loyalty turned out to be the one test I failed miserably.

Leadership, or the appearance of it, was another thing I could no longer assume comfortably. The usual respect my friends accorded me now seemed difficult to bear. One day, in between classes, Lan and Ting asked me to stand between them in the schoolyard. They squatted, put their hands and arms below my hips, clasped their hands onto each other's arms, stood up, and began to carry me around.

Normally, this human contraption would have impressed me. Not this time. Across the schoolyard I saw the boy who had led the martial arts group riding in a similar man-made carriage held up by two of his male friends. Lan and Ting had obviously seen the boys' contraption and had decided to replicate it. Most likely, they thought that if the boys could carry their friend around like a star, the girls could certainly do the same.

Much to my friends' disappointment, this girl was in no mood to play. As the boy looked my way from his carriage, I panicked. The last thing I wanted to do was to compete with him, for anything. The real competition, unintentional though it may have been, had already taken place and had made clear who could better lead the students of our class. He had won, hands down. I was not going to dispute the results.

"Let me down. Let me down, right now," I protested to my friends. "Don't worry," they assured me. "You won't fall. We promise." They began taking steps toward the boy's carriage. To them, it seemed like just another innocent game on another innocent day at school. I had no idea what they had in mind once the two carriages met, but I adamantly did not want to find out. "No, no, no, I don't care. Let me down. I don't want to ride in this thing." I started to shriek, "Don't go over there!" My protests worked. Lan and Ting put me down, puzzled that for once, I did not want to play along or compete with the boys. I hurried away and did not explain.

Not explaining did not make life less miserable. Toward the middle of the school year, Teacher Wang decided to make some routine changes to the seating chart. When she was finished, the leader of the disbanded martial arts group no longer sat on the other side of the classroom. Instead, he sat behind me.

From his new seat, he got to watch my every move. I continued to ignore him and he continued to say nothing. Weeks passed before I could tolerate his silent scrutiny no longer; I turned around and started talking to him. He seemed surprised but he responded. Initial awkwardness gave way to small talk and small talk soon turned into a habit. Before we knew it, we chatted regularly. I did not bring up our martial arts group and neither did he.

This newfound familiarity did nothing to alleviate my guilt. One day, after he joked at my expense, I hit him really hard. I had meant to tap him on the head in jest but my hand hit him with much more force than I intended. I immediately regretted it and wanted to apologize. I could not. Any of the other boys in the class would have hit me back, but he was not going to do the same. As I watched him flinch from the pain, I saw him standing in the front of the classroom again, supporting my assertion that I was not part of his "gang." Then as now, he took the hit, with no reward, no complaint, and no knowledge of all of the guilt and gratitude I could not find words to express.

Finally, near the end of the school year, I could no longer tolerate myself, so I groveled for forgiveness. We were sitting in a mostly deserted classroom during a break between classes. Most of the other students had left and gone outside to play. "I'm sorry," I turned around and said quietly. I had never apologized to anyone with equal sincerity. I could not be sorrier about abandoning him and our martial arts group, I continued.

He looked surprised, as if he had never believed an apology was necessary or would be forthcoming. Was the captain of the class beyond reproach? Or was this captain a girl who did not need to apologize to him?

As I proceeded with my apology, he looked at me intently, his surprise disappearing. "Thank you for what you did," I added. He might have done what he did because he believed it was the right thing to do. I could no longer behave as if I deserved it.

A hint of a smile broke across his face and he said something like "It's okay, no need to thank me." He continued to look at me intently, as if there was more that he wanted to say. But he said no more. As far as I was concerned, he had said all that I needed to hear. Groveling was not my forte—being captain meant rarely making mistakes that required an apology. But I desperately needed his forgiveness. He had now formally granted it.

Despite her tirade and her disbanding of my "gang," Teacher Wang remained my favorite instructor. I knew, however, that though I had imagined myself fit to be the heroine of any story, the hero of *my* story turned out to be the boy standing alone in front of the classroom.

Chapter Four

Leaving

The third grade came and went. My class made its way to fourth grade and moved into a new classroom, which, thankfully, was not next to the little boys' room. I remained the captain of the class and Teacher Wang remained our teacher. The boy who had led my "gang" continued to sit behind me, and though I no longer tortured myself with guilt about our gang incident, I continued to find his scrutiny somewhat unsettling.

Liang, another former "gang member," sat next to me. We talked a lot. He was a bubbly, mediocre student with a lot to say. I remembered him from our rooftop martial arts practices but never spoke to him about the shameful incident. When we chatted in class, we stuck to random topics. Whenever we conversed, we often turned our heads back to talk to the boy behind us. In general, he talked much less than Liang or I.

Liang was an only child and became the lens through which I viewed China's one-child policy. Though the policy had been implemented in 1980, I thought little about it until I read a story in a children's magazine. In the story, a boy insulted another boy who was an only child by using a funny line. The next day at school, I was determined to make use of my new knowledge. Turning to Liang, I asked, "Hey, do you have any brothers and sisters?"

"No," he answered without suspecting my motives.

"Really, you're an only child?" I asked despite already knowing the answer.

"Yes."

"Do you know what happens when you're an only child?"

"What?"

"Well, you become a selfish person who hogs everything, like money and food," I smiled. "And when you fart under the covers in bed, you'll hog that too, all by yourself! Haha."

I saw a smile creep onto the face of the boy behind us, and I laughed even harder.

"That's not funny!" Liang protested. "I don't fart in bed."

"Everybody farts."

"Then you're the one who hogs your own farts in bed."

"No, I'm not, because I'm not an only child. Haha."

"Shut up, you're so annoying."

"When children in China grow up in the future, they are going to be the only child in their families, and they're going to be just like you: smelling their own farts under the blanket. Haha, hahaha." I was now laughing uncontrollably, especially since the boy behind us had started laughing too. I could not have been more pleased with myself.

From then on, every time Liang tried to make fun of me, I reminded him that he was an only child who hogged his own farts under the covers. When Liang got annoyed, the boy behind us always smiled, and I always became immensely pleased with myself.

———

As much as I enjoyed my friends, I looked forward to leaving them for good. I was going to America, sooner or later. My father had three brothers who lived in the United States. Desperate for a life better than the one China offered, they had each made an illegal trek to Hong Kong decades ago and from there had made their way to the United States. In the pictures and letters they sent back to us in China, my family learned of their lives and of everything we did not have—their houses, cars, and electronic appliances.

When China reopened itself to the world and permitted its citizens to emigrate overseas, my family quickly applied to reunite with their relatives in the United States. Early in my elementary school days, my grandmother left for the United States. Next, the two uncles with whom my family shared an apartment left. Grandpa at first refused to go. He wanted to spend his old age in his own country, his own home. Grandma wrote to him from the United States and reminded him that everyone else had left or would be leaving China. If he stayed, he would be entirely alone, without any children or grandchildren to look after him. So when I was in third grade, Grandpa left for the United States, too. By 1985, my parents, my brother, and I were the only ones who remained in our two-bedroom apartment.

We were eager to leave. Like most of the other people in our city, my parents did not know much about America; they did know that China was poor and backwards. Each month, they stood in line along with their neighbors to purchase oil, rice, meat, and other staples using the ration stamps allocated to them by the government. After China initiated economic reforms in the late 1970s, their choices of material goods expanded, but despite these improvements, my parents remained unconvinced that life in Guangzhou could ever rival the quality of life in America. At one point, I overheard Mother say that the Chinese government could turn back the clock and unleash hell upon its citizens at any minute. Besides, she hoped to provide her children with an opportunity she never had: a college education. For me, things were a lot simpler. I just wanted everything that America had, including more food, better ice cream, more stylish clothes, and fancier toys. America held the key to my dreams.

During elementary school, my parents regularly visited the U.S. Consulate to submit documents, sit for interviews, answer questions, or inquire into the status of our application. If Mother came home crying, I knew that my new life would have to wait a bit longer.

————

Even as we waited for permission to immigrate, I was

having plenty of fun in Guangzhou. I had my friends at school and my brother at home. I even had an adult playmate: Mother's little sister. She lived in the same cluster of residential buildings as my family. Running from my building to hers took less than a minute. For me and my brother, her residence was a second home. Compared to our parents, she enforced fewer rules and supplied more candy and more fun.

My aunt lived in a one-bedroom, ground-floor unit that her father (my maternal grandfather) had purchased with his life savings. Though he was no longer alive, his and his wife's black-and-white portraits hung prominently in the living room. A container of burnt incense sticks stood in front of the portraits, demonstrating the respect the living paid to the dead.

My maternal grandfather had never learned to read or write, and had passed away before I was born. At age fourteen, before the founding of the People's Republic of China, he left the poverty and violent chaos at the end of China's last dynasty and made his way to Indonesia. There, he founded a small taxi enterprise, met my grandmother, and built a family. In the late 1950s, he returned to China with his wife and children. He escaped Indonesia's massacre of Chinese-Indonesians in 1965, but in exchange, he lived through the famine of the Great Leap Forward and the political chaos of the Cultural Revolution. The Chinese government showed him that Chinese leaders were just as capable of massacring Chinese people as anyone else.

Over the years, three of my grandfather's children left for Hong Kong. When my mother was eighteen, her mother passed away. Her father had spent what remained of his savings to try to cure her illness. My mother married a man who lived in the same neighborhood and moved out. A few years after my brother was born, my grandfather became ill, too. By then, there was little money left to attempt a cure for him.

My mother and my aunt often recalled how happy my grandfather had been when he held my brother in his arms, and unlike my paternal grandfather, he did not mind that his grandson made noise or created chaos. Mother and Auntie believed that he would have been just as thrilled with me.

Despite the pain and agony that transpired in my grandfather's home before I was born, it was now my sanctuary. My aunt made it so. It was the place to which I ran when I was bored, when I wanted more junk food than my mother would allow, or when I was upset with my brother's latest effort to snatch my toys. Also, my aunt regularly took us to all the places we liked: the playground, the park, the ice creamery, and the toy store.

As Guangzhou continued to welcome people, goods, and money from the West, my aunt avidly explored the new products and entertainment options in our city, often with her niece and nephew in tow. She took us to the Friendship Store, which sold Western products not available elsewhere; the arcade in the fancy hotel that catered to Western tourists; the restaurants that served Western cuisine; and the skating rink that played Western music.

Single and in her twenties, she eagerly donned the new women's clothing and beauty products that had made their way to Guangzhou from the outside world.

With boundless curiosity, I regularly participated in her discoveries. I was there for the first pair of heels, the first tube of lipstick, the first pair of stockings, the first bottle of perfume. I felt her excitement, her hope of becoming a prettier woman, her giddiness at the prospect of leading a more colorful life. I was not always content just to watch. So I draped her dresses onto my small body and walked around her living room in her heels, impatiently waiting for the day when I, too, could make myself prettier.

I could tell that my aunt loved all things from Hong Kong, and all things American. With every new product or piece of clothing she obtained, my aunt seemed to grow a little happier, and I grew to like Hong Kong and America a little more.

But Auntie longed for the world beyond Guangzhou much more than I knew. She dated a man who lived in a town on the outskirts of our city. My mother objected. Everyone in China wanted to move from the countryside to the city, and everyone on the outskirts of Guangzhou wished they were inside the city limits. Life was better in the big city, and no one from Guangzhou ever wished to leave for the less sophisticated, less developed towns nearby. Auntie would have no future with the man that she was dating, Mother told her. Auntie did not listen, insisting that he had relatives in Hong Kong, that he would leave China soon and take her with him.

Unfortunately, Mother turned out to be right. The man's brother was ill and sought treatment at a Guangzhou hospital. His town did not offer the same level of medical care. Auntie's boyfriend needed a place to stay while caring for his brother, and hotels in Guangzhou were far too expensive for his budget. So he stayed with Auntie. After she helped nurse his brother back to health, her boyfriend left for Hong Kong and decided not to take her with him. Auntie was left with no boyfriend and no one to bring her to Hong Kong legally.

At one point, she tried to go illegally. The trek from Guangzhou to Hong Kong included a strenuous swim across turbulent waters (at night) and a long trek through rocky terrain (before dawn). Chinese guards lined the border, ready to detain all those who dared to leave for the world of the capitalist running dogs. Even if one avoided the guards, he could not always avoid an encounter with the vicious sea creatures. Regardless, numerous citizens of Guangzhou and elsewhere made the journey. Many made it across; many others did not. Some never returned.

Auntie attempted the trek but never succeeded. She turned back when it appeared too dangerous. Fortunately, she was not detained by the authorities or torn apart by sharks.

My aunt's failure to escape China left her depressed, but I knew nothing of her desperation to leave or her great unhappiness. Perhaps she did not look forward to a lifetime as a factory worker in a state-owned enterprise, performing the same tasks over and over again for the rest of her life. On occasion, she asked my brother if he would be sad if she died. She never asked me. I was younger and likely would not have given her the reassurance she sought. After all, she once asked if I liked her more than an uncle in the United States whom I had met only once, and I said no, because my uncle lived in America and America was better. She spent the next hour lecturing me, telling me that she has done much more for me than my uncle ever had. I did not understand why the woman who loved America was not letting me love it in my own way. It did not matter. I relented, corrected my answer, and my aunt forgave me.

———

A month or so into my fourth grade school year, Mother returned from a visit to the U.S. Consulate. She was not crying. So I asked, "Are we going to the United States?" "Do you want to go?" she smiled. "Yes, of course." "Then we'll go. We leave in one month." "Really? Yaaaaaaaaaaaaaay!" I jumped up and down and ran around my apartment.

That evening, my aunt came to see us. She was happy for us. She could not leave with us, but in due time, we could bring her there, too. That would take many years, but we did not mind. One day, we would all be reunited over there. By now, Auntie had married a man who would not desert her. She was nearly thirty when they married, older than most single women in China. But she had a baby with her husband, and she was finally happy.

At school, I told Teacher Wang about my big news. During the years when we were waiting for America to let us in, Mother had instructed me not to share any information about our pending emigration. She did not want others to be jealous, or to gloat if we could not make it out of China. Teacher Wang was immensely happy for me. "That's great news, Ma Ying," she said, "but we will all miss you so much."

From that point on, school provided nonstop excitement. Teacher Wang announced to the class that I would be leaving and decreed that everybody, without any exceptions, had to turn in a picture that she would include in a photo album made just for me. Additionally, every student was instructed to give me a farewell present.

In the middle of the commotion I had caused, Liang asked me, "When will you come back?"

I turned toward him, and the boy behind us. "I don't know, maybe when I'm really old, like in my thirties. Maybe never."

"Never? So how are we going to see you again?"

"Maybe you can come see me in America."

"I don't think so; I don't know how to go to America."

"Hmm, then maybe you can't. It's hard to go there. It took years for our immigration application to be approved."

"Wow, we might never see you again? Will you miss us?"

"Of course," I said, pondering for the first time the prospect of never seeing my friends again. I felt a heightened intensity from the gaze of the boy behind us but was too nervous to look back.

"We'll miss you too!" Liang said emphatically, as if speaking for both himself and his friend. I stopped talking and turned away from them both.

Following Teacher Wang's decree, all of my classmates purchased gifts for me. On my last day at school, Teacher Wang threw a party. She presented me with an album of my classmates' photos, and my classmates offered their gifts. One student gave me a silver-tone pen accompanied by a silver-tone mechanical pencil. They were the fanciest writing instruments I had ever owned. I decided immediately that that I would use them in school in America every day.

I would never become super-captain, but in exchange, I would get America. I waved goodbye to my friends, my teachers, and my school. I exchanged addresses with Lan, Ting, and others, and promised to write. I did not cry—America was going to be great; I could not wait!

My aunt sent us off. Because there were no direct flights to the United States from Guangzhou, we took a train to Hong Kong. My aunt stayed on the train with us until we were at the Chinese-English border. She could not accompany us on our new adventure. I started to cry as she disembarked, but without her, our train rolled into Hong Kong.

Part II

The Ghetto

Chapter Five

Ghetto America

I threw up in a bag. It was my first plane ride, my first descent.

My stomach protested against the turbulence, but even vomiting could not dent my excitement. In a few minutes, the plane would land at San Francisco International Airport, and my family would be in America, at long last.

We had been waiting, hoping, and longing for America for years. When our plane landed and I stepped onto American soil, I eagerly looked around, hoping to find clues to my new life. I saw none, or at least none that I could understand. All the signs were in English and everyone spoke in a foreign tongue. I clasped Mother's hand, believing that she and my father knew, as they always had known in China, where to go and what to do. The fact that my parents spoke only a few phrases of broken English did not shake my belief. Mother looked nervous as she instructed me and my brother to stay close.

At a customs checkpoint, I waited anxiously as my parents attempted to answer numerous questions and complete multiple forms that they did not fully understand. Each of us was fingerprinted and issued new documents.

Then a customs agent questioned us about the contents of our luggage.

"Do you have any fruits?"

"No," my father answered.

"Any vegetables?"

"No."

"Any herbs?"

"What?"

"Herbs?"

"Sorry, no understand." My father looked lost. Mother looked concerned.

The customs agent repeated her question, but this time, in broken Chinese.

"Ah," my father looked relieved and switched to Mandarin. "You speak Chinese!"

"A little bit. Any herbs?" the agent continued in Mandarin.

"No," my mother responded.

"Let me see, I think maybe we do." My father scratched his head and began to open our huge blue sackcloth bag. Our belongings—clothes, photos, medicine, and everything we had thought we would need for life in America—spilled out. After a few minutes of observing my father rummage through his luggage, the customs agent appeared ready to let us go. Then my father reached deep into the bag and took out a box of dried citrus peels.

Our agent informed us in Mandarin that the item was not allowed.

"Okay, sorry," my father said in English and laughed. "Thank you."

The agent smiled and responded in Chinese, "Thank you."

My parents then stuffed our possessions back into our giant sackcloth bag. The customs agent cleared us and we were on our way into the United States.

As soon as the customs agent was out of sight, Mother said, "Why did you tell her about the dried citrus peels? She was ready to let us go without inspecting our luggage. She clearly liked you because you spoke a few words of English. Then you had to dig out the box."

"Well, she asked us if we had any herbs and we did," my father attempted to defend himself.

"You didn't have to tell her! She wasn't going to check. Why are you so stupid? You always have to tell people everything. That was a really expensive box of dried citrus peels and it was a gift. We could have used it to make soup."

My father shrugged. He probably agreed, but it was too late. The dried citrus peels were gone. We were now officially admitted into the United States. With or without our dried citrus peels, our new life began.

An uncle greeted us at the airport and shepherded us to Oakland, a city on the opposite side of the bay from San Francisco. There, a roomful of uncles, aunts, and cousins waited with my grandparents to welcome us to America. They had set up an apartment for us and we would share it with my grandparents.

As soon as we entered our new dwelling, my grandmother embraced my brother tightly, hopping up and down. He had always been her favorite, and he hopped with her. "My grandson is here! My grandson is finally here!" she declared. "I'm so happy. I've waited for you for so long!" Grandma let go of my brother for a second, then embraced him again as they continued to hop up and down together.

The daughter of a landlord, Grandma now worked as a babysitter. Long before her arrival in the United States, the Chinese government had confiscated her family's land in the countryside and their real estate in the city of Guangzhou. Grandma had adjusted to living without a driver, multiple maids, and lots of cash. America was another place to which she had to adjust. Here, she had to commute by bus, sometimes for hours, to change a baby's diapers and make it laugh. If her gray hair and wrinkles had multiplied, I did not notice, not in that moment of sheer joy when she held her favorite grandchild.

Grandpa must have been happy to see me, because I was his favorite. But Grandpa did not hop, and that did not bother me. No one else hopped either, but everyone seemed happy to see us. Finally, my grandparents' six sons and their families were all in America. My father had been the last of their children to arrive.

That evening, Grandma drew a bath for me. Grandma did not know what bubble bath was, but neither did I. It was enough that I had a bathtub full of hot water. Instead of sharing a squat toilet with the family next door, my family now had our own bathroom, complete with a sink, a flush toilet, and a bathtub. Best of all, I no longer had to take a shower in the kitchen. During my first few weeks in the United States, I spent hours in the bathtub each day. My family sometimes knocked on the bathroom door, wondering if I had fallen asleep. I had not. I just really enjoyed having an endless supply of hot water.

I had a bigger bedroom, too. I still had to share it with my brother, but unlike in China, we did not have to share it with my parents. They had their own room. Our family did not have the money to purchase a bed for both me and my brother, so we split the bed that was given to us by a relative: I slept on the mattress and my brother slept on the box spring. Neither of us complained. Our new beds were significantly better than the ones we had slept on in China, which had been made of wooden planks.

We also had a refrigerator, which meant that I could open the freezer and help myself to ice cream at any time. Unlike the ice cream in China, American ice cream was rich and creamy. My two favorite flavors were vanilla and chocolate, neither of which had been available to me in China.

We had access to many other new things, too: color television, carpeting, sofas, electric stovetops, heat, candy bars, potato chips, supermarkets, freeways, and much, much more. Eagerly, I looked forward to getting to know all the material goods my new country had to offer.

Two days after our arrival, when I was still waking up bleary-eyed in the afternoon from jetlag, my parents went out to look for work. Unable to speak English, they were in no position to be picky. So they accepted the menial work that was commonly performed by other Chinese immigrants who did not speak English. Mother became a seamstress in a sewing factory. Father worked at a fish market where he slaughtered fish and sea animals and stored them in a giant refrigeration room. They both worked a six-day week for less than minimum wage. They did not collect welfare and were not aware of any welfare or other social programs for which they might have qualified.

Instead of holding forth as the senior mechanic known as "Master Ma," my father worked as a low-level manual laborer whom Chinese colleagues and superiors frequently berated. He discovered that some Chinese immigrants derived great satisfaction from treating each other poorly. Instead of teaching reading and writing and inculcating moral values in a group of enthusiastic elementary school students, Mother now worked in a sweatshop, surrounded by women who hailed from China's countryside. Her new co-workers lacked her level of education but lacked no compunction about belittling her or each other.

While I soaked in my nightly tub of hot water, Father would come home with frost burns and open wounds on his hands and arms. He handled sea creatures all day long and even in death, they regularly stabbed him with their fins, tentacles, and claws. He talked and smiled a lot less than he had in China. Mother complained of not being able to sew as quickly as her co-workers. Her pay was determined by the quantity of garments she completed, but even after staring at the needle of a sewing machine for many long hours, she made little progress. She was much more easily agitated, and became inclined to scream at her children for the smallest offenses that we, naturally, did not consider offensive.

Father's new reticence and Mother's new agitation could not dent my excitement at getting to know my new life. But my new city looked nothing like what I had imagined. In China, I had thought that America was full of white people, but Oakland was predominantly black, and increasingly Asian and Hispanic. White people lived here as a racial minority, mostly up in the hills, where the streets were safer, the property prices higher, and the scenery prettier. They tended to be wealthier, better educated, and more polished than non-white members of the city's population. Other people—mainly poor blacks, recent Hispanic immigrants, and Asian people who spoke little or no English—lived in the wide swaths of city that stretched below the hills. Like my parents, many of them toiled in jobs they did not enjoy but had to keep, and lived in quarters that were too small but which they could barely afford. The rest of the country referred to these neighborhoods as "the inner city." I knew them as my new home.

All around me, I saw storefronts adorned with shattered windows, streets pockmarked with potholes, bridges and tunnels splashed with graffiti, and dilapidated houses clinging onto chipped paint and dangling wood panels. The streets near City Hall and the department stores downtown smelled of urine. Corner liquor stores attempted to keep out burglars, robbers, and vandals with iron window bars. Houses made feeble attempts to keep out unwelcome intruders with iron gates around their front yards. Run-down apartment buildings hosted residents whose personal belongings spilled out beyond their front doors, barely concealable in large trash bags.

The residents of Oakland surprised me, too. They included people who slept on the streets and did not go home. Many of them did not have homes. Some of them talked to themselves, cursing everyone who passed by their self-arrogated spots on the concrete. Others frequently approached my parents on the streets, extended their hands and demanded money. When we declined, they usually continued asking. At times, they followed us for a few steps or half a block; on other occasions, they yelled obscenities and racial slurs to which we did not respond. Then there were robbers, rapists, murderers, and other criminals. My parents made sure that I adjusted my life to their existence. For instance, I did not wander outside after dark. My grandmother reported instances when teenagers crept up to frighten her from behind as she strolled on the street in bright daylight or as she got off the bus in the dark. In the years to come, my uncles would encounter men who would beat them and forcibly take their cash or belongings.

Without any English language skills, my parents braved the streets of Oakland. In the early hours of morning and in the darkness of night, they waited at the bus stop for public transportation to take them to work or back home. They did not yet know how to drive, so they waited for the bus, for another long day to begin or end, for me and my brother grow older, for the burden of life in a new country to ease.

In their absence, my grandparents took turns bringing me to the hospital and the clinic to get the checkups and vaccinations necessary for school. Neither they nor I seemed to know for sure what we were doing. Supposedly, they spoke a few words of English. Since I did not speak English, I looked to them to explain to the doctors, nurses, and receptionists what I needed. Some of these professionals seemed as puzzled by what my grandparents were saying as I was. Grandma smiled and said "thank you" a lot. Grandpa sometimes wrote down the phrases that he was attempting to convey—he had always been a man of letters. All I knew was that my trips with Grandpa to medical facilities were far less exciting than our outing to Children's Park in Guangzhou. In the end, everyone seemed to understand enough to give me the medical care I needed.

———

With much trepidation, I went to school. I gave myself a new name. My uncles and aunts told me that it was a good idea to have an English name in America. So I chose the name Nina. On my first day of school, Ms. Washington, a tall, stylish black woman with a shaved head, introduced me to my new classmates. "Everyone, this is Nina," she said. Most of the thirty or so students in my fourth grade class were black. I looked at their unfamiliar faces with apprehension, but Ms. Washington's smile was very reassuring, and in her presence, everyone smiled and said hello. Soon enough, I smiled back.

Some of my classmates went out of their way to welcome me, perhaps because Ms. Washington had told them I was new to this country and instructed them to be helpful to me. The four or five Chinese girls in the class soon began serving as my informal translators and became my friends. A Filipina girl named Michelle greeted me with a big smile. At first, I thought she was Chinese, so I began speaking to her in Chinese. She quickly corrected my mistake with another big smile and the inability to respond in my language.

Many of my other classmates did their part to welcome me to America as well. On a bright, sunny California morning, I stood in front of home plate at a kickball game. Half of my fourth grade class was out on the field and the other half was behind me. I had never played or seen the game, nor did I speak enough English to convey that to my new classmates. After watching my dazed and confused expression for a few minutes, a slightly chubby black student named Marty left his position on the opposing team, jogged up to me and said, "C'mon, Nina, I'll show you." With his encouragement, I kicked the ball; the opposing team stood still, waiting for his lesson to run its course, and this boy to whom I had never spoken grabbed my hand and led me on a run from base to base around the field. When my feet touched home plate, I had scored my first point in kickball, sort of. My classmates on both teams cheered. Marty ran back to his position on the other team.

Soon enough, though, I learned that in the ghetto, friendliness and decency could be in short supply. Not long after my first kickball game, I sat across the table from three black students. They began to laugh and tried to decrease their volume, but they simply could not suppress their excitement. They looked at me furtively, looked at each other, and then laughed gleefully.

It was my second or third week attending school in Oakland. I sat in a large room full of screaming children. Teachers working in the city's public schools were on strike. School had been canceled. Instead of reporting to our respective classrooms, students from my school showed up at the church across the street, where a small number of teachers offered instruction for half a day. Ms. Washington and her reassuring smile were nowhere to be found. A blond, middle-aged woman who served as a temporary supervising instructor assigned me to a table where the three black students were sitting. She left me with various math exercises and quickly left to tend to screaming children elsewhere.

I looked at the three boys, who appeared to be a year or two younger than I. I had never seen them before. I took out the silver-colored pen and pencil set I had received as a farewell present in Guangzhou. Holding the pen in my hands, I rummaged through the papers the blond instructor had given me. A few minutes later, the boys sitting across from me started to laugh. I wanted to ask what they found so amusing, but I did not know how. So I decided to plunge into my math exercises. As I reached for my mechanical pencil, I noticed that it was no longer there. I looked around. The three students kept laughing, but now they were fighting over something. As one of them snatched something out of another's hand, I saw a flash of silver. Then I realized what was so funny: they had taken my pencil while I was not looking. There were three of them and only one pencil. Naturally, they fought over their loot.

Incredulously, I stared at all three students. I frantically searched for English words to condemn their theft but came up with nothing except more rage — I still did not know how to say "give it back!" I became effectively dumb, and in a matter of seconds, my rage, with nowhere to go, turned into tears. For a brief moment, the three students stopped laughing; then they collected themselves and began to laugh louder. Now that I had discovered their offense and could do nothing, they had no more reason to suppress their volume.

I stood up, wiped away my tears and sought the help of the first Chinese classmate I could locate. A few tables over, I stopped Cindy, who sat next to me in Ms. Washington's class. In an explanation made disjointed by shock, I asked her to report the incident to our supervising instructor. Having arrived in the United States only a year earlier, Cindy's English was about as disjointed as my request, but it was still leaps and bounds better than mine. Immediately, she accompanied me to see the middle-aged blond woman. I stood listening to them both, my eyes red and swollen.

Upon hearing our complaint, our instructor rushed to confront the three thieves. From a table away, I watched her chastise them, her face and words seemingly stern. Almost in unison, the boys pointed at me and screamed, "She's lying!" As the boys denied their theft without shame or hesitation, Cindy kindly translated. A few minutes later, the instructor returned to explain that she was very sorry but that there was nothing more she could do. I looked at her, somewhat dumbfounded that she would not punish the three boys. They would not be held responsible for their actions, and no one would be accountable for my loss.

"I am so sorry," the woman apologized again.

She handed me a stubby yellow No. 2 pencil and with an exaggerated, sad facial expression to signal her sympathy, she conveyed through Cindy that she hoped her pencil would compensate for my loss. Then they both walked away.

Neither the instructor nor Cindy had understood. They thought I had raised a fuss over a regular pencil. When chastising the thieves yielded no apparent results, the instructor did the next best thing—providing me with an item that she believed to be of equal (or equally little) value. Lost in translation was the fact that my pencil was shiny, metallic, and a hundred times superior to the cheap No. 2 pencils that nearly everyone else at school used. The three students had stolen my pencil precisely because they believed theft to be their only viable path to ownership.

I was bigger than all three of the boys. I could, and should, have seized my prized possession by force, but I had never beaten anyone to get what I wanted. In China, theft had almost never happened to me, let alone theft this brazen. Every one of my former class-

mates understood stealing to be shameful and potentially illegal. Our parents and instructors repeatedly
condemned it. Those who disobeyed were severely
punished with public reprimands in class followed by
potential corporal punishment at home. Sometimes,
the innocent were punished along with the guilty, but
I was a model student who was never presumed
guilty. I had never placed any item in plain sight in a
classroom in China and feared its disappearance. Even
when my instructors imposed edicts I did not understand, as when Teacher Wang disbanded my martial
arts group, I did not lose my trust in the authority fig-
ures in my life.

In the ghetto, however, I could not count on my
classmates to know right from wrong, nor could I
count on the adults to ferret out fault and dispense
punishment. Standing in a church with less than a
month under my belt in this new country, I clutched a
stubby No. 2 pencil that I did not want, far away from
my friends who would have never subjected me to the
same display of shamelessness. Instead of my former
classmates' familiar faces, I now saw panhandlers who
refused to take no for an answer, thieves who stole my
belongings, and thugs who harassed my grandmother.

I hated the three thieves. I hated their poverty,
which had inspired them to covet my possession and
conspired with them to take it from me. I hated their
parents, who had failed to teach them that being poor
was no excuse to steal. I hated myself for not adequately guarding an irreplaceable gift and for not
doing all that I could have done to retrieve it once it
was gone.

School ended soon after the theft. On my way home, my tears began to well up again. A block away from my apartment, I stopped. My parents and Grandma were at work, and my brother still had not returned from school. Grandpa was likely the only one home. He was too old to work and spent much of his time at home. He seemed lonelier and more fragile than he did in China. Here, he was without his long-time friends and acquaintances, without partners with whom to practice Tai-chi, without a variety of Chinese magazines and newspapers to keep him company. I did not want him to worry. I took a deep breath and wiped away the tears. If this was what my new life in America was going to be like, I was determined to stop crying and get used to it.

That evening, long after my tears had dried, I told my family about the theft.

"Don't worry, we will buy you another pen and pencil," Father tried to reassure me.

"You can't," Mother interjected. "That set was irreplaceable. She got it as a gift from her little friends in Guangzhou. It had great sentimental value."

"Man, she was just stupid," My brother chimed in. "She should have never taken her eyes off of her belongings."

"I'm not stupid! How was I supposed to know that they would steal my stuff?" I protested loudly, but I couldn't help thinking that my brother was right.

"You couldn't have known," Mother tried to comfort me. "I can't believe your teacher didn't do anything about it. Next time, be more careful. Just remember, people can steal anything from you anywhere, any time."

I nodded. She did not have to remind me. I was already determined to remember that, forever.

In a few weeks, the teachers' strike was over and I eagerly returned to Ms. Washington's classroom. I had missed her reassuring presence. I believed that under Ms. Washington's watchful eye, my first encounter with shamelessness in the ghetto would never have happened, or would not have happened without the thieves receiving their proper punishment.

I was right. Back in Ms. Washington's classroom, no one stole from me. Nevertheless, my classmates frequently demanded from me that which I had no obligation to give. Every time I consumed a snack, whether it was a bag of peanuts, a candy bar, or a few M&Ms, my classmates, including those I did not know well, always wanted a share.

On a sleepy afternoon, I opened a bag of dried mango slices on the playground. Readily available in Oakland's Chinatown, dried mangoes emit a faint aroma of the fresh fruit and offer the sweet taste of added sugar. Like many other products of the developed world, they were not available in China. I considered them one of the rewards of my journey to the United States. Standing next to Cindy, I popped several slices into my mouth.

Melissa, a chubby girl from my class, stood nearby. Immediately, she walked over and asked, "What is that?"

I shrugged. By now, I spoke enough English to understand her question, but "dried mangoes" was not yet part of my English vocabulary. It did not matter.

"Can I have some?" Melissa asked.

I popped a few more slices in my mouth. I barely knew Melissa and did not want to share. In China, my classmates did not brazenly ask others for food. We all believed that such behavior reflected bad manners.

"Can I have some?" Melissa repeated herself.

I did not know how to politely decline. Besides, my instructors in China had taught me to share generously. Reluctantly, I gave Melissa a few of slices of my dried mangoes. She happily walked away.

"Nina, what did you give Melissa?" Minutes later, Tyesha, a tall, skinny girl who sat in front of me in class, stood before me. She and Melissa often played together on the playground. Because Tyesha sat in front of me, I spoke to her far more regularly than I did to Melissa. Due to my language constraints, much of what we said included simple greetings and a smile. Nevertheless, Tyesha had not hesitated to raise her hand in class a few weeks before to inform Ms. Washington with great urgency, "Nina just said a bad word!" She had overheard me converse with the Taiwanese boy next to her.

"She does not even speak English," Ms. Washington replied.

"She said it, I heard her!" Tyesha insisted.

"Nina, did you say a bad word?" Ms. Washington stopped the class and asked.

I looked confused, as I did not know what a "bad word" was. Cindy, who was sitting next to me, translated the question.

"No," I responded, still confused. I then informed

Cindy that perhaps what I said in Chinese was not the most elegant, but it did not count as a "bad word." In any case, Tyesha did not speak Chinese and could not possibly have understood what I said. The Taiwanese boy who sat next to Tyesha agreed.

"What did you say?" Cindy asked in Chinese.

"*Fang gou pi*," I answered. I was accusing the Taiwanese boy of spewing dog fart.

"Ooh, Ms. Washington, Nina just said it again!" Tyesha screamed before covering her mouth in shock.

Cindy said something to Ms. Washington in English.

"Nina, you should not say bad words in Chinese either," Ms. Washington said to me, as Cindy translated. I disagreed that I had said a "bad word" in Chinese. Cindy had conveyed the wrong message to our instructor. Regardless, Tyesha clearly believed that I had said something else. But because Ms. Washington seemed ready to move on from the incident, I thought it useless to argue the fine points. So I nodded.

Now, on the playground, Tyesha inquired about what I had given Melissa. I shrugged again. I still did not know how to say "dried mangoes." Once again, it did not matter.

"I want some. Can I have some?" Tyesha asked.

"No," I shook my head. I was already regretting sharing my snack with Melissa. I did not want to give any more of it away.

"C'mon, give me some! You gave some to Melissa."

Once again, I shook my head.

Tyesha stomped away, screaming angry words.

"She just said something horrible about you," Cindy noted.

"I don't care. It's my snack, not hers," I said. "If she wants it so much, she can ask her parents to buy some for her." I offered some of my dried mangos to Cindy and rapidly ate the rest.

I could not understand why Tyesha felt entitled to my food. As far as I was concerned, I owed her nothing. I was just as poor, if not poorer, than the rest of my classmates. Our collective poverty was evidenced by the fact that we, along with nearly everyone at my school, took advantage of government-subsidized lunches for children of low income families. Still, I did not walk around demanding food from others. My classmates clearly felt differently and often approached me for snacks in the way that Melissa and Tyesha had done. Over time, I learned to eat my snacks quickly at school, before anyone else could make demands on them, or to eat them at home.

———

My most pressing priority was learning English. I left my classmates each afternoon to attend a small English as a Second Language class with four or five other recent immigrants. Back in my own classroom, I sat through lessons in science and social studies without having any idea what was going on. I excelled in math, though. The math lessons consisted of material I had already learned in China. I found it strange that my classmates were so behind, and stranger still that they spent so little time studying. Even the worst student in my class in Guangzhou studied harder than most of my classmates in Oakland. Ms. Washington sometimes asked me to help my fellow students, such as Tyesha and Melissa, with math. I gladly did so.

My brother had his own way of learning English. In very little time, he acquired a vast vocabulary of profanity. For months, he came home from school with new four-letter words or new ways of using them. Excited about every new find, he appointed me his student. I did not object. Together, we learned to curse. Each time I learned a new insult, we laughed uncontrollably. Our parents were usually not around to hear us, but even if they had been, they would have had no idea what we were saying.

During the second half of the school year, I began to participate in some of Ms. Washington's grammar lessons. I did not always understand fully what she said, but I did not always have to. I just needed to follow her directions. For instance, when singular or plural nouns were followed by verbs, I did not always need to understand what the nouns or verbs meant. I only needed to add "s" or "es" to the right verb. When I completed her grammar exercises properly, Ms. Washington always seemed delighted.

In my second semester, when I answered a grammar question that a few of my classmates could not, Ms. Washington stopped the class. "Very good, Nina," she said, "and she's only been in this country for six months." For the next few minutes, she lectured my classmates. I did not understand all of what she was saying, but by the stern look on her face, I could tell that she was exhorting her students to work harder and pay closer attention in class.

The following year, my fifth grade instructor, Mr. Ridge, would make a habit of highlighting my good study habits to shame the students who underperformed in his class. A boy named Theo often liked to mumble something in protest, and it almost always enraged Mr. Ridge. "Theo, all you ever do is complain. Oh, I can't do this. I can't do that. And you always have excuses: I'm tired. I'm not smart enough. I want to watch TV. Let me tell you something. You're just lazy and you don't apply yourself. Do you see Nina saying that she forgot to do her homework? Does Nina tell me that the work is too hard? She's got the same assignments as you, and she's only been in this country for a year." At this point, Theo would stop protesting because he knew that if he said any more, Mr. Ridge would just continue to reprimand him.

Mr. Ridge was a middle-aged black man who appeared less approachable than Ms. Washington. Yet just like her, he was always delighted when I did well. He even tried to give me individual math lessons. It was obvious to him that my math skills were superior to those of my classmates, and on a couple of occasions when my classmates were out on the playground, he attempted to teach me the subject at a more advanced level. When I completed the math exercises correctly, he liked to say, "Yeah, you got it, you got it!" But our individual sessions did not continue. He was very ill and was absent for long stretches of time. When he returned, one of his big toes had been amputated to keep his illness from spreading.

Mr. Ridge's deteriorating health did not stop him from exhorting Theo or other students to do better, or from getting upset when he discovered that the substitute teachers had not sufficiently looked out for my interests. Each year, my school organized a camping trip for fifth and sixth grade students who performed well in class and were well-behaved. That year, a substitute teacher selected five or six students from my class for the trip. Because I did not speak English well, I did not make the cut. When Mr. Ridge returned to the classroom, long after the camping trip had ended, he made his displeasure known. Repeatedly, he said to his class, "Nina should have gone to camp." I was grateful for his concern, but I did not wish to go camping anyway. My parents would have had to pay at least fifty dollars to fund my expenses for a week, and it was money that I did not want them to spend.

In any case, learning English remained my number one priority. Due to my language deficiencies, I brought a small English-to-Chinese dictionary to class each day and attempted to broaden my vocabulary by looking up words I did not understand. I also continued to rely on my Chinese friends for translation assistance. Cindy was not in my fifth grade class, but most of the other female classmates from fourth grade were. Despite my need for their assistance, we had little in common. Like the rest of my American classmates, they ate far too much junk food and spent too much time watching cartoons on television.

In Mr. Ridge's class, they refused to let me work with them on a science project, using the excuse that their group was already too big. Later, one of the members revealed the real reason: two of the Chinese girls who spoke the best English felt that I would have nothing to contribute to a project that was language-intensive, and no one else objected to their decision. After all, the others had to rely on these two girls to do most of the work.

In the end, Tyesha convinced her group to accept me as an additional member. She seemed as upset that my Chinese friends excluded me as she had been when she believed that I had uttered a four-letter word in fourth grade. This time, I was immensely grateful for her interference. Her group was even larger than the one my so-called friends had formed. When the science project was complete, our science instructor singled out our group for high praise. I did not gloat, and continued to rely on my Chinese "friends" for translation help, but I actively looked forward to the day when I would no longer need it.

———

I read voraciously in Chinese, searching for a China that no longer belonged to me. I drowned myself in martial arts novels to which I had no access in Guangzhou but was now able to borrow from the library in Oakland's Chinatown. During my first summer in America, I spent nearly all of my free time on the couch, immersed in multi-volume Chinese martial arts novels that wove stories about ambition, power, love, and betrayal before a backdrop of kung fu, dynastic rule, and political insurrections. My brother did the same. My father attempted to shoo me outside to play, but I refused. He did not have time to inspect my books to see whether they contained too much violence, too much sex, or too much moral ambiguity for a child. They did, but with my parents stuck at work for long hours and my brother burying his nose in the same books, no one was going to stop me from reading spellbinding stories that were inappropriate for my age.

Besides, my parents were too busy trying to improve our lives in America to pay attention to what I was reading. By this time, we had moved into our own apartment and were no longer living with my grandparents. My parents had graduated to slightly better jobs, too. Father became a kitchen helper at a Chinese-owned restaurant. Instead of frostbites and stab wounds, he came home with burn marks from the hot stove or grill. The verbal abuse from his new employer, however, was no less intense than the abuse he had received in his first job in America. Mother continued her work as a seamstress at a sweatshop, but she found various odd jobs "on the side" that paid more. My brother and I now each had a bed instead of half of one.

But our poverty was sinking in. We purchased our clothing from Goodwill and the flea market, or we accepted hand-me-downs from friends and relatives. We used donated furniture, electronics, and appliances as well. We could not afford to purchase all the snacks I wanted to eat. So I always salivated at everything I could not have in the candy and snack isles of supermarkets.

Meanwhile, my brother and I both began to assume more responsibilities at home. In the early days, my brother continued his mischief-making, but that did not last very long. Perhaps he knew that he could not and should not go on with his pranks. Perhaps he saw far more clearly than I the fatigue my parents brought home. Perhaps he understood better all that they did not say: each day, their employers treated them as if they were subhuman. They were quickly forgetting what it felt like to be treated as respected professionals in their own fields. They were even beginning to forget what it felt like to be treated like normal human beings. Perhaps my brother also noticed that I was too young to understand and felt a need to shoulder some of the family's responsibility. Increasingly, he became more serious, though from time to time he succumbed to the lure of troublemaking. I could tell, however, that he was losing his joy.

Despite everything I was too young to understand, I decided to help bear my family's burden too. In fifth grade, I began to cook dinner every evening. I did not really know how to cook, but it did not matter. Much of my cooking involved the simple tasks of steaming, boiling, frying, or making rice in a rice cooker. Mother often prepared the more complicated dishes for me to heat or reheat at dinner time.

I started to clean, too, and began to do everything from sweeping the floor to washing the dishes by hand. Eagerly, I took on and performed household chores that had not been assigned to me. This made me feel like a grownup.

After school, I took my parents to the hospital when they were sick, accompanied them to the unemployment office when they were laid off, made the necessary phone calls when we needed phone service, gas, or electricity. When letters arrived from the bank, the government, or advertisers, I read them. If a utility company overcharged us, I called to dispute the charges. When insurance companies sent explanations of benefits, I read them with the help of a giant Chinese-to-English dictionary. My brother performed similar tasks.

There was a community center in Oakland's Chinatown that offered services to recent immigrants like us. My parents could have brought all their mail and English documents there to be translated, but the translation service would have cost them a small fee. Some years later, my father would attend a free job training program at that community center, and attain a higher-paying job as a machine operator for a fireplace equipment manufacturer. For the most part, however, my family eked out a living without much help from the state.

At first, the tasks I performed for my parents seemed daunting. I started out tentatively as my parents' interpreter and shyly relayed their requests and wishes. As my English became more proficient, I became more confident and more impatient. Over time, wherever I took our parents, I yelled at every government bureaucrat, receptionist, waiter, or shopkeeper who treated them rudely because they did not speak English or discriminated against them because they were Chinese. As my profanity became increasingly useful, my parents urged me not to be so insolent, but it was too late. They could no longer speak on my behalf as they had done in China, and their inability to speak for themselves meant that I could no longer maintain my silence.

———

I performed well enough in fifth grade that Mr. Ridge recommended me for a sixth grade class that was the only class at my school designated for "gifted" students. I was likely the only student for whom Mr. Ridge made that recommendation, and I was fortunate that he picked me. My English had improved dramatically, but it was still shaky. I continued to excel at math, but overall, I could not have been Mr. Ridge's best student. He probably recognized that of all his fifth graders that year, I was the most eager to learn. Though he could not send me on a camping trip, he made sure that I would study in the most academically rigorous class at my school. Sadly, he would pass away a couple of years later from his illness.

In sixth grade, I continued to diligently refer to my Chinese-to-English dictionary in class, but I was no longer a new immigrant for whom other Chinese students had to perform translation. In fact, none of my female Chinese classmates from fifth grade made it into my "gifted" class. My new classmates enjoyed a reputation for being smarter than everyone else at school, but I found them to be more mean-spirited and less friendly. They were also wealthier: fewer of them qualified for government-subsidized lunches than the students in my fourth or fifth grade classes. Regardless, some of my new classmates shoplifted. An obese white girl named Joy—the only white person I knew who lived in a worse neighborhood than mine—stole from me when she visited my home. By now, I no longer cried about it.

In sixth grade I got rid of the name "Nina." I desperately wanted to hold onto my Chinese name. After all, this was the name I had used at a different time, in a different place, when I was a different me, when my city did not violate me with its ugliness or threaten to swallow me with its brokenness. I was already changing almost everything to equip myself for life in America. I was not going to give up my name, too.

Chapter Six

Letters from Guangzhou

During my first year in the United States, Guangzhou lived vividly in my mind. Repeatedly, my city appeared before me....

In the morning, Teacher Wang began the day's lessons. Liang and I mumbled to each other when she was not paying attention. The boy behind us looked on.

At mid-morning, the entire school took a break. Children screamed and ran around the playground.

At the end of the day, we filed out of the main gate to patriotic tunes, wearing red scarves issued by our school. The color red symbolized the blood spilled by the heroes of the People's Liberation Army to liberate our country. On the way home, Ting relayed the latest tidbits she had gleaned from newspapers.

In the late afternoon, school was out. There were no screaming children, no one at play, no mayhem, no mischief. The schoolyard silently bore the sun's blazing rays. Every now and then, a breeze gently ruffled the tree leaves, and a bird unenthusiastically flapped its wings. At home, I fought and argued with my brother.

In the evening, I had dinner with my family. If Mother gave me permission, I ran to my aunt's apartment, asking for candy and snacks, admiring her new clothes or beauty products. When darkness fell, I returned home. At night, I slept soundly on my bed made of wooden planks, stirring only when trains sped along the railroad tracks near my apartment, blaring loud sirens and blinking bright lights.

———

From the ghetto, I wrote to my friends in Guangzhou. At first, I shared with them my excitement about being in America. They wrote back quickly, wanting to learn more. When my excitement dissipated, I found myself having less to say—it was difficult to explain how incredibly different my new environment and my challenges were from theirs. I also gradually began to see the futility of our letter-writing—after all, it was likely I would never see them again. Over time, my responses became more sporadic, and I left some of their letters unanswered. My friends did the same. Perhaps they were getting as accustomed to my absence as I was to theirs.

In fifth grade, I received a letter from Lan and Ting. We had not corresponded for several months. In the letter, they beseeched me to write to the boy who had led my martial arts group. He had started smoking, was skipping school, and may have joined a real gang. He refused to listen to anyone who advised him to change his new habits, but according to my friends, he would listen to me. "Here is his address," they wrote. "Please, please tell him to stop going down the wrong path. He cannot continue this way." Lan and Yi had never co-written a letter to me before. In their request, they said nothing about the incident in which Teacher Wang had disbanded my "gang," but they did not have to. We had all been present. For days afterwards, Yi had reminded me that the boy had saved me from Teacher Wang's wrath. Did they now think that I could save him?

I read the letter several times. I knew I was supposed to tell the boy to return to school, reject truancy, and walk away from the temptations of juvenile crimes. I did not know how. He was the boy who had led half of my class, even without an official title. Perhaps once, as captain of his class, I had felt entitled to instruct him on how he ought to behave. Not anymore. Not after he saved me, as the leader of my "gang." I did not know how to save him from joining a real gang, but I tried anyway. I wrote to him and asked him how he was. I told him that I hoped he was doing well in school, that school was important, and that he could write to me any time.

He never did. I waited. Weeks passed. I wondered if he had had trouble convincing his parents to give him the money to pay for overseas postage. Then months passed. Still his letter did not come. I stopped waiting. It was no use. The sooner I stopped missing my friends in Guangzhou, the sooner I could move on with my new life. Shortly thereafter, I stopped writing to my friends.

———

I did not, however, stop writing to my aunt. She wrote to my family from Guangzhou. She did not have a telephone at home, and though we did, we could not afford to make international calls except on rare occasions. So my aunt and my mother exchanged letters. In letter after letter, Mother conveyed news about her children's performance in school, her latest squabbles with her in-laws, the humiliations she and her husband suffered at work, and the frustrations she could not share with her young children. My aunt wrote back, often in equally long letters, conveying the joys and challenges of motherhood, the disagreements she had with her husband, the facelift Guangzhou was undergoing, and her steadfast support for my family as we faced the difficulties with which our new land presented us.

When a letter from my aunt arrived, our whole family read it. I did not always understand every word. My fourth-grade education from China had not fully prepared me for written conversations between adults, but I always understood my aunt's sentiments. Often, she wrote a few extra lines at the end of her letters addressed to me and my brother, encouraging us to do well in school, learn English quickly, and listen to our parents. Those words I always understood perfectly. Every now and then, I would write her a letter to tell her what and how I was doing. In return, I would receive an entire letter addressed just to me.

I looked forward to my aunt's letters. They offered encouragement and gave me strength. I never told her about the ghetto, but I did not have to. I was sure she understood.

One day, a different kind of letter from my aunt arrived. Mother read it and walked away with tears in her eyes. After she left the room, I picked up the letter.

More than usual, the letter contained words and phrases I did not know. My aunt had been in the hospital. Some kind of procedure had been performed on her. She had not wanted the procedure but she had not been given a choice. It was mandatory, and no amount of bribing or begging could get her out of it. Then it happened.

I read the letter again. I noticed numerous words about medical instruments and how they were used on her. The hospital took something from her, and she would never be able to get it back. She did not sound angry, just sad and powerless. There was no recourse, no remedy. Despite all the words I could not comprehend, I understood her grief perfectly. Before I knew it, I, too, had tears in my eyes.

On many occasions, I had counted on my aunt to share my joys and dispel my sorrows. In her great moment of sadness, there was nothing I could do. I could not even fully understand who or what had inflicted such great harm on her and why.

Years later, I would realize that my aunt had had a forced abortion. The one-child policy that I had once joked about with Liang was not funny after all. When my aunt became pregnant with her second baby, the state took it away from her, with no second thoughts, no regrets, and no apologies. My aunt lost a baby, and I lost a cousin.

Her letter told of the horrors of China that I did not yet understand, but the horrors of the ghetto were staring me right in the face. Battling them would require all the strength I could muster.

Chapter Seven

"Chinaman" Gets into a Fight

My racist classmate was right in my face. I could see her spit flying as she said, "You Chinese bitch, I'm gonna kick your ass."

I was in seventh grade in the ghetto. I hated my school and my fellow students. The walk to junior high school took less than fifteen minutes, but it always felt like an eternity. Each morning, I dreaded the walk and walked slowly. I was never late, but I always tried to delay my arrival, even if only by a few minutes. I hated the frequent violence, the constant racism, my shabby clothing, and the shallowness of adolescence.

I was hungry to learn and stood out academically. I took "gifted" classes, but because I was too advanced for my school's "gifted" seventh grade math curriculum, I took math with eighth and ninth graders. The summer after sixth grade, my brother had given me a used algebra textbook and told me to study it. I followed his advice. I was no longer his little tail, but I listened to every word he said, now more than ever.

Our parents could not guide me in school, so my brother took it upon himself to fill the void. Upon entering seventh grade, I took a math test and was placed in algebra and geometry. Many of my fellow seventh graders were still learning long division.

Math had not been my favorite subject in China. I had mastered it well enough but never enjoyed it as much as the reading and writing that Teacher Wang taught. In America, math was the one subject in which I had a comparative advantage. I did not hesitate to use it to distinguish myself academically.

The following year, I would skip the eighth grade and take advanced classes that my junior high school did not offer—a chemistry class at a high school in the morning and advanced algebra and trigonometry at a community college in the evening.

Most of my classmates seemed to think I was strange. The eighth and ninth graders with whom I took math classes appeared to resent me. In class, I often answered the questions they could not and scored better than they did on exams. I wore thick glasses and was not interested in their adolescent games or their flirtations with one another. Some of the boys would smirk whenever I raised my hand to answer a teacher's question. Some of the girls would laugh at the clashing colors and the ill-fitting clothes I wore, often not bothering to lower their voices.

As far as my older classmates were concerned, no one should have been studying as hard as I was studying. I thought differently, believing what I had been taught in China: hard work and academic excellence could lead to great things.

No one told me that stellar grades in the seventh grade did not count toward college admissions or toward life in general. My parents knew nothing about the American school system. None of the adults at my school counseled me to enjoy my teenage years instead of burying my head in books and equations. My instructors and counselors had bigger problems to worry about: students who toted weapons, engaged in drug use, participated in gang activity, or got pregnant.

Besides, I wanted to study. Unlike many of my fellow students, I enjoyed learning. I had few friends and did almost no socializing outside of school. Other girls my age gossiped incessantly. I was not interested. They obsessed over makeup and hair. I did not have the money for the former or the patience for the latter. They constantly talked about and shopped for new clothes. I wore secondhand items purchased from Goodwill or given to me by friends and relatives. Some of my classmates liked boy bands; almost all listened to popular music. I knew nothing about American music. Everyone else loved movies and television and idolized celebrities. I had never been to a movie in America and considered celebrities and celebrity worship moronic.

My school, like my city, was predominantly black, increasingly Asian and Hispanic, and barely white. Racism, which had been a minor issue in elementary school, was a constant presence in junior high. Numerous black students regularly screamed racial epithets at their Asian counterparts. "Ching Chong," "Chinaman," and "Chow Mein" became our names.

Sometimes, our tormentors imitated the way in which we spoke our native tongues. On other occasions, they physically assaulted us or threatened to do so. No one ever doubted who would win in a fight.

Along with other Asian students, I did my best to avoid physical confrontation—those who openly and regularly uttered racial epithets always appeared ready to back up their threats with violence. When black students made fun of the "Chinamen" among them, I said nothing. When they screamed at the middle-aged Cantonese cafeteria aide and called her a "stupid Chinaman," I, along with all the other Asian students present, pretended we did not hear anything. When they routinely threatened to beat up their Asian classmates, who were generally smaller in size, I looked away.

Racism did not end at the school fence. On the streets of Oakland, black teenagers regularly hurled racial insults at adult Asian immigrants who spoke limited English. One common tactic was to creep up behind an elderly Asian person and frighten him or her with sing-song nonsense, such as "Yee-ya, ching-chong, ay-yahhhh!" Meanwhile, numerous black adults discriminated against Asian immigrants at the grocery store, on the bus, at the hospital, the unemployment office, and everywhere else. Each time I witnessed such behavior I gritted my teeth, felt a burning rage, and watched the racism take place in silence.

If ever my rage burned so hot that I felt compelled to respond, the compulsion would quickly cool when I inevitably noticed the embarrassing fact that the other "Chinamen" nearby—Chinese, Vietnamese, Koreans,

Filipinos, and anyone else who looked Asian—were deliberately ignoring my anger and the incidents that caused it. Just as frequently, I found myself ignoring incidents of racism against other Asians. Physically, we were usually no match for those who discriminated against us. Culturally, we were predisposed to be less confrontational than our non-Asian peers. Collectively and individually, we chose to remain silent when faced with physical threats and verbal insults. Conscious of our own shame, we rarely discussed this physical and verbal abuse amongst ourselves. After all, our collective humiliation was there for all to see. In our failure to act, to defend ourselves, there was nothing to discuss. What were we supposed to say? "I'm sorry I could not defend you, but I don't know you and I was not going to risk my own safety for you." And what does one say in response? "It's okay, I understand; I would not have stepped up for you either." In the end, what most Asian students did was to speak pejoratively about their abusers among themselves, in their native languages. Each time, I wanted to ask the speaker why he did not have the courage to stand up to those who assaulted or insulted him. But since I lacked that courage myself, I never asked any questions. I just loathed our choice, our shame.

On the whole, the Hispanic students at school treated Asians with less hostility than the black students did. Nonetheless, many of the Hispanic students who spoke English joined the black students in bullying and discriminating racially against Asians. The more recent immigrants, however, did not speak enough English to engage in racial slurs. Like many

Asian immigrants, they wore shabby clothing and came from impoverished families trying to eke out a living. They spoke Spanish and tended to congregate among themselves. Every now and then, I spent time with them. Maybe our immigrant experiences unified us, but our language and cultural barriers, as well as the discriminatory behavior of other Hispanics, always kept me from becoming a close friend to any Hispanic student.

Meanwhile, the large Asian student population at school provided me with little comfort. Although I ate lunch each day with a few Chinese girls, we did little else together. I felt I had little in common with my Asian peers. While many of the other Chinese students could not read or write Chinese, I regularly immersed myself in Chinese text. Those who could read Chinese often preferred to discuss the appearances of actors and actresses from Hong Kong and other subjects I found trivial. I could never bring myself to join them in these conversations. The Chinese language represented my link to four thousand years of history, high culture, and intellectual achievement. I was too young to fully understand that long history's full glory or its modern-day tragedies, but I knew that my cultural heritage consisted of much, much more than mindless conversations about Asian celebrities and shared silence before racism.

For a similar reason, I rarely socialized with Chinese students who were born or grew up in America and spoke little or no Chinese. These students tended to cluster together; their ignorance about China and Chinese culture was vast but their knowledge of

America seemed unimpressive. For some of them, my ability as a recent immigrant to excel beyond them, not just in math and science, but also in language-intensive classes like English and history, created an extra source of annoyance. A number of the Chinese girls who had been my "friends" in fourth and fifth grade attended junior high school with me. But I had broken away from their circle, and we no longer spent time together. Many Asian students seemed to think I was stuck up or unfriendly, or both. I did not expect them to understand.

The white students at school made up an extremely small minority of the student population, but along with certain Asian students, they were always present in the small number of "gifted" classes the school offered. I thought of them as a curiosity; although many of them were cordial and polite, I found little to talk about with them. Most of the white students lived a much more sanitized life than I. While I lined up each day, along with much of the school, for government-subsidized lunches, most of the white students brought or bought their own. While I lived in an apartment on a crime-strewn street, they mostly lived in neighborhoods where the grass was greener and the streets safer. They talked about movie stars, boy bands, and shopping, and I found their conversations uninteresting and uninspiring.

Becoming friends with the few black girls in my "gifted" classes turned out to be much less cumbersome. They did not subject me to the racial slurs, physical confrontation, or derogatory comments that I had frequently faced in the schoolyard. By inner-city standards, they were quite nerdy. The following year, my American history instructor would praise one of them as the only person out of his "gifted" bunch who could write a decent essay. I often found myself more comfortable with these girls than with my white or Asian classmates. Perhaps our nerdiness brought us together. Perhaps both they and I were different from others who shared our respective races.

Then one day, I forgot about my relentless pursuit of academic achievement, my attachment to Chinese culture, and my inability to relate to my peers. I had a decision to make: Was I, or was I not, going to remain a "Chinaman"?

A Hispanic girl named Maria was right in my face, and I could see her spit flying as she threatened, "You stupid Chinese bitch, I'm gonna kick your ass!"

Just minutes ago, we had been sitting on the floor mats inside a small room. We were in the middle of gym class. Our instructor had been telling us that we would play basketball among ourselves that day. He would disappear and leave us unsupervised, as he often did. No instructor at any of the schools I had attended in Guangzhou would have ever contemplated walking away from a class while it was in session. In the ghetto, it was a daily occurrence.

Right before the instructor sent us outside that day, I heard someone growl, "Moooove, you Chinaman. You're in my way." I looked behind me. Maria was talking to me. The floor mat was filled with students and she wanted more space. I hesitated.

"Bitch, moooove," Maria repeated her demand.

"No, you move," I responded with neither certainty nor conviction. Confrontation was not my forte.

Maria did not share my compunction. Like many others at my junior high, she showed up at school but did not learn; she went to class but did not study. She liked to present herself as a "badass" who was ready to fight her way through any disagreement. Yet she rarely picked fights with students who were larger than her in size. Instead, she preferred to dish out racial slurs to those who looked Chinese. Against us, her epithets rarely elicited a response.

She was now becoming visibly agitated. "Listen, you Chinese bitch," she threatened. "If you don't move, I'm gonna make you." I did not move.

Her first punch landed on my right thigh, a couple of inches above the knee. I saw the muscle twitch. Before that moment, no racist had ever physically attacked me. Up until then, I had always managed to stay quiet or walk away.

I punched back. Then she hit me again, and I responded in kind.

I was no stranger to fistfights. At home, periodic scuffles with my brother, who by now was some thirty to forty pounds heavier than I, had continued after our arrival in America. Getting hit by a girl who was not much bigger than I was entirely unremarkable. There was, however, something deeply unsettling about being in a fight at school. Fistfights were for punks, gangsters, and losers who would amount to nothing good, not for a super-nerd with a 4.0 grade point average.

The students in our gym class started to file outside. I got up to leave as well, hoping that would end the scuffle. It did not. Maria followed me. Her usual posse, which consisted of about three other Hispanic girls, surrounded us. Racial slurs started to fly.

"Yeah, kick her Chinese ass!" "Chinese bitch!" "Stupid Chinaman!" Maria's friends egged her on.

Maria took this cue and again got in my face. She would stay there for the rest of the class, taunting and cursing me. Every now and then, she would attack physically. Each time, I would respond, but without equal fervor.

Whenever Maria attacked, her friends would cheer and yell more racial epithets at the "Chinaman." When she engaged in trash talk, they would laugh. Throughout the confrontation, others came to watch and then went away. Not all of them were her friends, but none was mine. Perhaps my friends did not know what was happening. Perhaps they did know and just chose to stay away. I had few friends anyway.

Michelle, the Filipina girl whom I had known since Ms. Washington's class, was my only friend who was nearby during the fight. We were not particularly close, but we had remained friendly since fourth grade. She had always been kind to me, and to everyone else. A few days before my fight, we ate lunch together in the school courtyard. Instead of throwing away her soda can, she saved it for the older Asian man who scoured the campus each day, hunched over with a large bag, to collect cans and bottles for recycling. When Michelle handed him her soda can, a couple of black students in the courtyard shouted in his direction: "Hey, Chinaman, come here and take this!" I winced. Michelle said nothing, and neither did

I.

Out of the corner of my eye, I saw Michelle at a basketball court that was within earshot of every word uttered in the fight, but she did not look our way. With her back turned toward us, she tried again and again to shoot a ball into the basket. She would stay there repeating the same motion, by herself, for the rest of the class.

I felt the cold wind as it blew through my thin white sweater. The fall semester was nearing its end. The damp California winter was approaching. Frigidity was creeping into my limbs, interrupted only by a kick, a punch, or a slap from Maria.

"Man, her braces hella stink," Maria said, continuing with her trash talk.

I had to continue with mine: "You look like a fucking mummy," I replied. Trash talking was not a skill I had practiced regularly during the three short years I had been speaking English. Without even thinking about it, I invoked the latest topic in my world history class. We were in the middle of studying ancient Egypt.

Someone watching from the sidelines murmured, "What's a mummy?" The target of my insult, however, understood the reference perfectly. She had good reason to. Like many other female junior high school students in the ghetto, she wore heavy and cheap makeup. It added a thick layer of brown to her face and made it look lifeless. This brown goop was accompanied by extremely dark eyeliner that made her eyes look hollow. Her bright red lipstick accentuated the lifeless appearance of the rest of her face and revealed a mouth full of braces.

"What did you call me? I don't look like a mummy. You're the fucking mummy, you Chinese bitch."

"Go fuck yourself, you Mexican ho." The audience gasped. No one blinked when blacks and Hispanics, or anyone else, insulted Asians with racial slurs, but since Asians rarely responded in kind, or at all, my response was scandalous. In the seventh grade, standing alone on the basketball court, this was the only response I could muster.

My racial slur sparked another physical scuffle that ended when Tyesha, another classmate from elementary school, placed herself between me and Maria. By now, Tyesha stood an entire head taller than I. Laughing and facing me, she blocked me from hitting Maria. Then she turned to Maria and blocked her from hitting me. Still laughing, Tyesha advised both of us to stop fighting.

When neither Maria nor I showed any interest in heeding her advice, Tyesha seemed even more amused. After a few moments, she left us to find entertainment elsewhere. Tyesha did not persist in her attempts to break up the fight, but the brief moment when she stood between me and Maria—when she did not exactly take my side and in fact prevented me from hitting anyone—offered me a tiny respite from feeling entirely alone. With Tyesha gone, I returned to the trash talk and physical confrontation. Nearby, Michelle was still shooting hoops with her back turned toward us.

The fight continued until the bell rang. Maria and her friends decided to go to their next class. So with a bit more trash talking and jeering from the sidelines, they left.

Michelle was now gone from the basketball court too. There was little she could have done had she stood by my side. She would have risked being physically attacked herself. Like most Asian girls, she did not swear, rarely yelled, and never traded racial insults. She looked just as Chinese as I and befriended mostly Chinese classmates. Once, I had mistaken her for someone of Chinese descent. The remarks from Maria that had started the fight could have been uttered to Michelle just as easily as they were uttered to me. But they were not. So she pretended she was not there. I never forgave her.

I slowly walked to the locker room to change clothes before my next class. My hands were numb from the cold. In the frigid autumn air, no other Chinamen seemed to share my rage, even as they daily shared my humiliation.

Incredulous friends and acquaintances approached me throughout the rest of the day. Many asked, "You called her a Mexican ho? Why?" Upon discovering my reasons ("because she called me a Chinese bitch"), their incredulity gave way to either confusion or bemusement. A pretty Asian girl in one of my "gifted" classes looked as if she wanted to ask why that was worth fighting over, but she must have seen the fatigue in my eyes, so she just walked away. I vaguely recalled that she was sitting quite close to me when Maria demanded more space on the floor mat in gym class. Joy, the obese white girl who had stolen from me in elementary school—and who now regularly resorted to racial epithets against Asians—nearly broke out in laughter. She did not, perhaps because she still needed to copy my homework for our next class.

No one asked if I was physically hurt. I did not report the incident to any of the school's instructors or administrators. I did not believe that they would have cared or done anything useful.

Like a zombie, I floated from class to class for the rest of the day. When school ended, I slowly dragged myself home. As much as I hated junior high school, I never rejoiced on the way home. On most days, outrage and bitterness accompanied me. On that day, I had chosen not to be a "Chinaman," but the result made clear that I was just a foul-mouthed nerd who got into fights she could not win.

Perhaps if I had had more "friends" like Michelle, or more friends in general, I would have felt more normal, more content, and perhaps I, too, would have wondered why rejecting "Chinaman" as my name was worth fighting for. But I was not a normal adolescent. Unanchored to strong friendships or carefree pursuits, I firmly held onto my ethnic pride. In elementary school, I reverted to my Chinese name. In junior high school, I got into a fight.

At home that evening, I did not discuss my fight. By this point, I no longer had to make dinner for my family every night. Mother was an assemblywoman for an electronics company and worked a normal eight-hour day. She had decided that I should spend more time on my studies and had taken over the cooking again. My other tasks—helping my parents live nearly every aspect of their daily lives by serving as their translator and advisor—remained. I no longer performed these tasks eagerly. They seemed endless. Performing them only made me resent the fact that "normal" teenagers did not have to bear the same burden for their families. Regardless, I did not want my parents to worry about a daughter who got into schoolyard brawls, whatever the reason. There were no bruises and no marks on my body, and no need for any explanation.

I did my best to appear chipper, and did such a fine job that my brother observed, "You seem really happy today. You must have had a good day at school." I mumbled an unintelligible noise and he took it as a "yes."

———

My brother had his own problems in high school. He took a few "gifted" and honors classes. The more advanced high school classes were clearly difficult for him, as his English skills had not yet caught up with those of his peers. Each night, he stayed up well past midnight, huddling in front of a giant English-to-Chinese dictionary to decipher the words in his Honors American History textbook or write essays for his "gifted" English class. What took him an entire night often took his American-born classmates no more than an hour or two.

I sometimes read his essays. He wrote about Guangzhou. I knew that he missed it more than I. He had been older when we left. He remembered more of it—his friends, his hotspots, his activities, his habits, his city. He also wrote about a pretty, athletic, and popular white girl on whom he had crush but whom he could not bring himself to approach. Unlike me, he spoke English with an accent. Just like me, he wore shabby clothing. He had no chance with the girl and he knew it.

The constant racial slurs must have angered him even more than they did me. He had never shied away from a fistfight in China. On the rare occasions when he had not been not strong enough or fast enough to prevail, his friends had stepped in on his behalf, and he had had more friends than anyone. America was different. Most of the Asian boys preferred to keep their mouths shut when insulted or discriminated against. My brother was not used to keeping quiet, but his new city had new rules. His own size and the racists' numbers were against him. I would not have been surprised had he found it difficult to abandon completely the code of honor that he had once followed in China, but if he did get into fights, he never told me or our parents about them.

Some weeks after my fight, I encountered an acquaintance from one of my "gifted" classes in the ladies' room during our lunch break. As we stood in front of the mirror, she noticed my drab facial expression and asked with exaggerated concern, "You are not happy either?" I shook my head and asked, "Why are *you* not happy?"

She tugged at her shoulder-length blond hair. "My hair on the right is curly at the ends but my hair on the left is straight," she explained and made a sad face.

I looked at her hair, and noticed only a minute difference between the strands on the left and those on the right. In the past, I would have at least pretended to sympathize, but not that day. To me, her privileged life was an annoyance, her hair a poor excuse for being unhappy. I walked out of the bathroom without acknowledging her plight. She did not notice, and continued to fret in front of the mirror. I was pretty sure I hated her, too.

Chapter Eight

The Sky Is the Limit

I stepped into the shower. My parents had already gone to bed. I was exhausted but relieved to be enjoying my first moment of peace in months.

"Police, open up!" Men were yelling outside as they pounded on my neighbor's door.

I turned off the faucet. There was more pounding next door, and then more yelling: "Police, open up!"

The door opened, and the policemen burst in. Commotion followed, but I could not make out the specifics. I thought about putting my clothes back on, just in case. But in case of what? I did not know. My neighbors could jump the fence into my backyard. The police could pursue them on a hot chase, or pound on my door. Whatever the scenario, I knew I would be better off with clothes on. Nonetheless, I stood still in the bathtub, straining my ears to hear the muffled voices from next door. No one screamed. No shots were fired. After about five minutes, the policemen left. I could not tell if they had taken anyone with them.

I waited as the police cars drove away and faded into the night. Silence returned. I turned on the faucet again.

It was my family's first night in our new house. Five years after we immigrated to the United States, we bought our first house. But we bought what we could afford and moved from a bad neighborhood to a worse one. The visit from the police to the house next door was our big welcome.

The next morning, I said nothing about the incident to my parents. Sooner or later, we would all discover just how inhospitable our new neighborhood was, but there was no need just yet for any unsettling news. First-time home ownership was exhilarating for my parents. They proudly took snapshots of the new house and sent them to friends and relatives in China.

Despite having walked my parents through every step of the purchasing process, I was in no mood to celebrate. I was in the tenth grade. My brother had graduated from high school and was working at a relative's Chinese restaurant in another state. I had been the only thing standing between my parents' deficient language skills and a real estate transaction's potential pitfalls. Purchasing our house had involved mountains of legal documents and paperwork. For several months, I pored over long and convoluted documents ranging from the termite report to the property appraisal. I endured a seemingly endless string of phone calls to real estate brokers, insurance agents, bank representatives, and others in order to clarify the terms and conditions of our purchase. I spent hours explaining my findings to my parents and advising them of their rights and obligations. Repeated reading rarely made convoluted documents seem less convoluted, and I worried that I might make a mistake that would cost my family in our biggest financial investment yet. Whenever I came across a question I could not answer by myself, I worried even more. As the transaction moved toward completion, my fatigue increased. On most evenings, I felt as if I could fall asleep standing up.

We had hired a Chinese real estate broker who was an immigrant herself and who went above and beyond the call of duty to assist my family with our real estate purchase. For several months, I showed up at her office and phoned her or her assistants to discuss the details of our mortgage and our real estate transaction. On some days, I spent more time speaking with her than anyone else, including my teachers and friends. She noticed my fatigue and meticulously shepherded my family to home ownership. She often explained documents to us several times, first to me and then to my parents. She accompanied us to meetings at which she did not have to be present. At our closing, she extended what would normally have been a short meeting for an extra hour and a half because she wanted to explain thoroughly to me what documents we were signing. I took notes; the representative facilitating the closing looked on impatiently. Afterwards, my family had a house.

On the night we moved in, I had a moment to take it all in, by myself. When the police showed up next door, I knew that our new house would not be a place of peace for us.

From the beginning, police officers regularly visited our neighborhood, but not nearly as often as crime and violence did. Gunshots rang, not every night, not every week, and sometimes not even every month. But they were there, sometimes distant and sometimes close. If a series of popping sounds interrupted our evening television programs, we just turned up the volume. When one morning my father discovered a bullet hole in the side of our house, he was not surprised.

A park tucked away at the dead end of our block was a haven for criminal activity, but frequently, the action spilled out into plain view on the street. Now and then, I had the dubious privilege of witnessing drug dealing or gangbanging from my bedroom window.

A liquor store stood at the other end of our block. Teenagers loitered in front of it every afternoon. Inside, they shoplifted. Outside, they talked trash, got into fights, and accosted passersby.

The beat-up cars parked on the street served as silent witnesses to the neighborhood's disarray and disgrace. More than a few of them looked on with broken headlights, flat tires, mangled frames, and shattered window glass. Their deformities showed off the neighborhood's poverty and its inhabitants' purposeful destruction.

I stayed off my front porch and avoided taking strolls after dark. Every once in a while, the police knocked on my door to seek information about crimes that had been committed in the neighborhood. My family never knew anything. The one time my father answered a question from the police about whether he had seen a neighbor's car parked on the street the previous evening, my mother yelled at him for not lying to avoid potential trouble. Luckily, whatever came of the police investigation, no trouble came our way.

———

Over time, our street became browner, but not less poor or less dangerous. After a couple of years had passed, the two-story apartment building that the police had visited on my first night in the neighborhood became almost entirely populated by Hispanic residents. We did not bother to socialize with them. The police still visited their building occasionally. Perhaps the reasons differed from before, but my family did not inquire. We had no interest in getting to know the people who were stuck in this unsafe neighborhood with us.

Our new neighbors offered up blaring music every weekend, starting early in the morning and lasting well after dusk. They also threw parties that caused hordes of cars to be parked everywhere along our block, on the curb, in front of our house, and sometimes in our driveway. On weekends and late afternoons, the children of the families who lived next door screamed outside, climbing over the fence into our backyard and horsing around on our front porch without permission.

When reprimanded, the children retaliated. One weekend afternoon, on my way out of the house, I instructed various children from next door to remove themselves from our front porch. They left unwillingly and unhappily, grumbling something in Spanish. When I returned at dusk, my parents stood on the front lawn looking forlornly at two sunflower plants they had acquired just a few days before. The plants stood almost six feet tall, one on each side of the small staircase leading up to our house's front door. When the sun shone and the giant sunflowers perked up at the top of the plants' stalks, it was as if our house found a reason to smile in spite of its awful surroundings. But someone had plucked off every single leaf from both plants, leaving nothing but two enormous discs on two thin sticks, looking ugly and naked. Instead of a warm smile, our plants now offered a freak show.

My parents said nothing. Gardening was one of the few hobbies they could afford, but they did not speak enough English to confront the culprits who had trespassed on and damaged our property, nor did they wish to risk confrontation with our sketchy neighbors. So they stood on the front lawn, their heads drooping like the damaged sunflowers they loved.

I, however, knew full well who the culprits were. They were standing around snickering. And for the first time, I marched straight into the building next door in search of the culprits' parents. Behind me, my mother yelled in Chinese, "Ying, come back! Let it go, you don't know what kind of people live there."

I was not listening. We had tolerated our neighbors' blaring music, their children's unwanted intrusions onto our property, and their guests' cars blocking our driveway. But I was not going to excuse this intentional act of vandalism. If the adults next door did not know how to educate their children, I was fully prepared to give them some instructions.

I walked up the stairs to the apartment in which the culprits lived, knocked on the half-opened door, and walked in without waiting for an invitation. Outside, the children lingered nervously. The space inside felt dark and cramped. Makeshift furniture vied for space with wrinkled clothing; used goods tried to edge out expired groceries. A small lamp lit the room dimly.

A middle-aged Hispanic woman emerged. Perhaps she had been in the kitchen or the bathroom, or perhaps she had just been standing in a dark corner of the shabby living room. She looked surprised to have a visitor.

"Hallo?" she greeted me with a thick accent.

"Hi, I live next door." I pointed in the direction of my house. Then, pointing at her children lingering outside, I said, "Your children tore all the leaves off my plants."

"What?"

"They tore...they broke my flowers. You can come see." I gestured for her to go outside and see for herself.

She seemed to understand as she screamed out the names of her children. Sheepishly, they entered the room. She asked them a question in Spanish; they offered a stuttered response in a fearful tone. "I'm sorry," she said, and before I could answer, she started to spank her children and to scream even more loudly at them in Spanish. The smaller of the children, a little girl, began to cry. The older one, a little boy, screamed something back at his mother, which provoked her to hit him harder. He ran away to the other side of the room. His little sister was not so lucky. Her mother had a tight grasp on her and she had nowhere to run.

"It's okay," I said, trying to interrupt the beating.

"So sorry," she apologized again. "No next time."

"Okay, it's okay." I tried to squeeze out a smile.

"They break again, tell me."

"Okay, thank you."

She screamed something at her children and they both reluctantly mumbled an apology in my direction.

"Okay, just no next time."

I thanked the mother again and quickly left.

I had never lived in quarters so cramped or dark or depressing. Then again, I had never vandalized anyone's lawn. It must have been difficult for my neighbor to subsist in a new country without English skills, without money, and with two trouble-making children by her side. My family had once fought a similar fight against poverty, against the lack of dignity, against the unknown. In many ways, we were still trying to claw our way out. On days like that one, I felt the absurdity of the need to fight against other immigrants like her.

Outside, our naked sunflowers beckoned me home, their damage reminding me of the reason I had barged into someone else's home. Back in my own house, I relayed the apology from next door to my parents. Then I told them to get rid of the sunflowers and to never again plant anything worth looking at or caring about. My parents sighed, but agreed. Then they advised me not to walk into strangers' houses by myself. I waved them off impatiently. Who would speak for them if I did not? I did not have the heart to say—or the patience to explain—that if they could have spoken for themselves, I would never have taken the risk I had just taken.

Each day, the ghetto chipped away at our pride and dignity as we quietly endured the sound of gunshots, the sight of drug dealing, and the ever-present threat of violence. I was not willing to live in fear of mere children, or to allow them to destroy my family's meager possessions with impunity. I was lucky. I had been wearing a mini-skirt from Ross and a pair of cheap high-heel sandals from Payless. I might have encountered a large, ill-intentioned man, but I had not. Instead, I just found an immigrant mother who did not hesitate to discipline her children.

After that day, I never again set foot in the building next door. Hispanic residents came and went from the property. Whenever a new family moved in, I had to instruct a new set of children to stay off of our property. Sometimes my admonition worked; sometimes it did not.

———

School continued to provide its share of ugliness. I used an uncle's address to get into a public high school in the hills that was the whitest and supposedly the best in the city. As it turned out, numerous other students at this high school did not live in its district either. Many of them had enrolled without a fake address. Each day, they took public buses up the hill from neighborhoods farther away from the school, far poorer, and more unsafe than mine. Somewhere between where they lived and our high school, the buses stopped and I hopped on. Together, we made our way up to a pristine and beautiful part of town that neither their parents nor mine could afford to live in. On our way up, we caught a view of the bay that divided San Francisco from Oakland. On clear days, we could even see as far as San Francisco. At first I imagined that we were leaving behind the grittiness of Oakland. In reality, we were merely bringing it up to the hills.

The buses were always packed with black, brown, and yellow people. The back of the bus belonged to the black students. Sometimes they were joined by Hispanic students, but never by yellow people, who always tried their best to stay away. The back of the bus never hesitated to throw paper balls, candy wrappers, assorted junk, racial slurs, and profanity at the "Chinamen" in the front or the middle. Perhaps once a week, the insults directed at me and the other female "Chinamen" included sexual remarks vulgar enough to make Howard Stern blush. When I looked around, I noticed that just as in junior high, the other "Chinamen" tuned out the insults by eagerly discussing Hong Kong movies and actors or by gossiping about their friends. I gritted my teeth, kept my rage in check, and said nothing.

Just as in junior high, the Chinese women who served lunch in the high school cafeteria endured racial slurs from insolent teenagers. A Chinese instructor was regularly called a "Chinaman" by nameless students in chaotic hallways. Asian students continued to face racial slurs and racially motivated bullying.

My high school was a little whiter than my junior

high, but not by much. Some of the white and non-white parents who lived in the hills sent their children to the public school in their district. Many others sent their children to private schools or to public schools in safer, nearby cities. Regardless, I now saw more white people than I had ever seen before. Instead of five or six white students in my classes, I now attended "gifted," honors, and advanced placement (AP) classes with as many as ten or fifteen white students.

My ability to excel in math dwindled in high school. My interest had begun to fade in ninth grade. By high school, I was burnt out. Nevertheless, I was reluctant to relinquish a subject in which I had once excelled. The most advanced math class at my high school was pre-calculus. So in eleventh grade, I took calculus in the evenings at a local community college. Somehow, I could no longer push myself to do well in the subject. A full load of honors classes was strenuous by itself. Coupled with my endless tasks at home, my course load felt even heavier. As I sat in my calculus class each evening, I felt the day's exhaustion catch up with me. I yawned, dozed off, and had trouble paying attention. I felt a certain amount of disgust, too, because the class was keeping me from going to sleep earlier at night. At the end of the semester, I received a grade of C. It was the first and only C I have ever earned. This was not supposed to happen to me, and definitely not in math. But it did. I regretted pushing myself to study a subject in which I had lost interest and wondered why I had not been content to learn it at a regular pace, like everyone else my age.

Thankfully, other academic subjects offered better

rewards. I had outgrown the fantasy world of Chinese martial arts novels. Literature and political philosophy filled the void; I devoured the stories that the former constructed and pondered the human condition that the latter sought to describe and improve. Instead of sword fights and kung fu, I immersed myself in Ayn Rand, John Steinbeck, J.D. Salinger, Thomas Hobbes, John Locke, Machiavelli, and the Federalist Papers. This world of ideas was as fascinating as the inner city was ugly. On the pages of the books I read, America revealed itself to me as a world beyond shattered windows and gunshots, beyond limitless ice cream flavors and well-stocked supermarkets. Despite all that I could not see or touch in real life, I found in my books the triumph of individualism, the senselessness of war, and the sanctity of the social contract. Each time I identified with a sentiment, found inspiration in an idea, or recognized a call to action, I felt an indescribable joy and became a little happier. Even though I still lived in a cramped and depressing ghetto, these books freed my mind, gave it wings, and allowed it to fly. At the same time, my fondness grew for the country that had made these discoveries possible. In the middle of a semester, I would sometimes realize that I was enjoying it slightly more than the preceding one. I was beginning to feel as if I belonged to my new country a little more than I once did. Guangzhou remained a fond memory, but it was becoming an increasingly distant one.

Moving up the "knowledge chain," however, was not without its challenges. In eleventh grade, I managed to enroll in the only Honors English class my school offered. Out of some six hundred eleventh-graders, about thirty qualified for this class. My instructor, Ms. Connors, a middle-aged white woman who lived with her boyfriend in San Francisco, regularly lamented the coarsening of American culture. In the fall, she instructed her students to write a report on American art.

I chose to write my report on the landscape paintings of the Hudson River School of the mid-19th Century. Inspired by the renditions of American landscapes and the spirit of early America prominent in the works of the School's most notable artists, I poured my heart into writing my best report yet. When I finished, my report totaled some forty pages. My fellow students, many of whom far less inspired by the subjects they had chosen, turned in shorter reports.

When the reports were graded, I received a B+. Many others in the class received an A, including those whose reports I had deemed less thorough, less articulate, and less worthy. Aghast at my grade, I confronted Ms. Connors.

"Why did I get a B+ instead of an A?"

"Well, your presentation was not as good as your classmates'."

"What do you mean?"

"Your entire report was handwritten. It just became too hard to read."

"There's nothing wrong with my handwriting. All my other essays have been handwritten."

"Well, those other essays were just a few pages long. Most of your classmates turned in type-written reports."

"I spent a lot of time on it, much more than those people who typed up their reports. I shouldn't have to type up my report to get a good grade"

"It just became too hard to read."

"You didn't even read it all?!"

"I'm not going to argue about this. Your presentation just wasn't good enough."

"Because my report was not typed?"

"Yes."

"So it made no difference to you that I actually appreciated the material and wrote a great report?"

"Look, I already said I'm not going to argue about this. I'm not changing your grade."

"Bitch," I grumbled to myself as I walked away. Ms. Connors did not hear me, but I was sure that I had not endeared myself to her with our latest conversation. There were more white people in that Honors English class than in any other class at my high school. Nearly every one of these students lived up in the hills and nearly every one of them owned a computer. I did not. While most of my classmates printed out their reports from computers, I handwrote mine. I had not expected that an instructor who was adamant about art appreciation would refuse to finish reading a report about art.

It did not help that Ms. Connors had tried to exclude me from her class. I was one of the few students she had not handpicked from her tenth grade English class. At the beginning of the school year, I turned in an in-class essay that I had not known would be graded. I had understood it as a mere brainstorming exercise. As a result of my mistake, I received a 3.5 out of 5, which inspired Ms. Connors to ask my tenth grade English instructor, Mr. Matthews, why he had recommended me for her honors class in the first place. She told him that I should be demoted to a lower-level class, but he firmly stood behind his original recommendation, insisting that I be given more time to prove my aptitude. Only much later did I notice that I was one of the few tenth graders he had recommended for Honors English. I had never considered myself to be one of his best students, but much like Mr. Ridge in fifth grade, Mr. Matthews showed an unwavering faith in my ability to hold my own among students who were performing at a higher level. I had handwritten every one of my essays for him, too, and he had never once refused to read them.

A more caring instructor might have offered me the chance to type my report and resubmit it, but Ms. Connors, not anyone else, was my English instructor. Even if I found it unfair and was unwilling to accept it, presentation always mattered.

A few weeks later, my brother returned home. Naturally, I complained to him about the incident.

"Everyone else in your class has a computer?" he asked.

"Almost everyone. How many other poor immigrant kids do you think take Honors English? Maybe a bunch of them show up in Honors Physics and Honors Chemistry, but only a few make it to Honors English."

"Someone else must have handwritten their report too. What kind of grades did they get?"

"Well, there was at least one other girl who handwrote her report. She got a B+ like I did, except my report was much more substantive than hers. It didn't matter, because that bitch didn't read it. Next time, I'll just fucking type everything on the typewriter."

"Forty pages is a lot to type."

"No shit, and it was forty pages single-spaced. That's why I didn't type the fucking thing in the first place. I would have had to write out the entire report and then type it on the typewriter. It took me forever to write it. But if I don't type it in the future, that bitch won't read it, and she won't give me an A."

"Yeah, I guess that means you'll have to type it."

Ever since we started speaking English fluently, my brother and I had often conversed in a torrent of profanity. By the time I reached eleventh grade, we were no longer just practicing. Our parents could not understand what we were saying and were in no position to insist on more polite language. After our conversation about the incident in Ms. Connors' class, my brother appeared deep in thought. He had just returned home from out of state. I assumed he was tired and left him alone.

A few weeks later, he bought me a computer. He could not have saved more than a few thousand dollars working at a Chinese restaurant, and after our conversation he spent about a thousand of that because his little sister had gotten a B+ on an English report. My brother had been accepted at a state university after high school and had attended for a semester. But he had tired of college quickly—three years of studying past midnight in high school had taken a toll, and he no longer had any interest in studying. In years to come, he would study at other colleges. For now, he shelled out what little money he had in order to support my academic performance.

Thanks to my brother's generosity, Ms. Connors no longer had an excuse not to read my work. The next semester, I earned an A in her class. The following year, she allowed me to proceed to her AP English class, which was the only such class my school offered. I had earned my spot, but I still disliked her. It did not matter that she dutifully exposed her students to great literature and helped them improve their writing. When she offered a class after school, without pay, to help her students' prepare for the verbal section of the SAT, I was grateful, especially since I could not afford a private tutor. But I continued to believe that the learning process in her class was a raw deal instead of a fair fight. For this I deeply resented her, even though I had never resented other, less conscientious instructors, including those who had not taught at all, or had disappeared from class each day. The summer after eleventh grade, I took an English class at a community college, in part to earn college credits before starting college, and in part because I wanted additional exposure to one of my favorite subjects. I was thrilled that my instructor was a kind woman whom I respected far more than Ms. Connors.

Perhaps in a more perfect world, my parents would have called Ms. Connors and reasoned with her on my behalf, but my parents did not speak English. They trusted my self-discipline and initiative, so much so that they had not bothered to look at my report cards since I skipped eighth grade. This system had worked out well for all of us. By the time I reached high school, my mother had joined my father as a machine operator at the fireplace manufacturing company. Each day, they stood in front of hot furnaces, casting iron and handling heavy machinery. My performance in school was one item they did not need to worry about. Furthermore, I would probably have been too impatient to describe what I was learning and far too angry to explain why I had failed to garner an A for a report in my Honors English class. As far as I was concerned, it was great that my parents did not ask.

My grandparents did not ask, either. They simply assumed that I did well in school. Grandma had now ceased babysitting for a living. She and Grandpa were both too old to work. Grandma found ways to entertain herself, whether by singing karaoke at the Chinese community center or by gossiping with her friends and relatives. Grandpa spent his days tending to the flowers on his balcony, feeding his goldfish, and reading and rereading Chinese newspapers and magazines. His reading options were limited, but his time was not. Unlike Grandma, he did not enjoy socializing. When I visited their apartment, I often found him sitting on his sofa and puffing on his pipe. The former chief civil engineer looked lonely and must have felt a bit lost in the country he and his wife had adopted in their old age. Whenever their grandchildren visited, though, the faces of both of my grandparents always seemed to light up. Before I became utterly disgusted with math, I told Grandpa that I wanted to study civil engineering in college and follow in his footsteps. He seemed to like that most of all. In his and my grandmother's presence, I caught fleeting glimpses of myself as a kid who enjoyed life and didn't have to struggle under the weight of schoolwork and family responsibilities. But I always extinguished such memories before they grew too strong.

———

In high school, I started working part-time jobs to earn spending money. I did not get much of an allowance from my parents, nor did I ask for anything that was not necessary. The summer after tenth grade, I got a job at one of Oakland's most popular movie theaters. The day I filled out my job application was the first time I entered an American movie theater. I got the job and would work as a cashier at the theater throughout my high school years. I had never heard of many of the items that Americans bought at the movies. The Goobers, Red Vines, and Raisinets I sold at the theater were far more expensive than the Twix, Snickers, and Kit Kat candy bars I purchased from the supermarkets near my house. I had never tasted popcorn, either. For the first few days at my job, I took time to study the candy drawers so as not to be lost when a customer made his order. Meanwhile, I learned to make and serve popcorn, all the while stuffing myself with it whenever I took a break.

I eagerly watched all the free movies available to me. Already, I was watching more television in high school than ever before. Originally, the goal of my TV-watching had been to perfect my English. But over time, the plethora of options on the small screen made me laugh and kept me entertained. At the movie theater, a new door to American popular culture was flung wide open. I walked in and embraced this new world. It was stupid, crass, funny, moving, and spellbinding all at once. I sat captivated, as I had done in China when my brother took me to see my first American movie, *Rambo*. Then as now, the silver screen brought me into a world that was neither drab nor depressing. By allowing myself to enjoy it, I began to understand why Americans always seemed so carefree, and I felt a little more American myself.

My colleagues at the theater were mostly black and Asian. Everyone worked together and got along. Racial slurs and resentment rarely surfaced at my workplace. My older colleagues looked after me like a little sister. The younger ones became my playmates. Going to work seemed like going to a big party. My co-workers often wondered where I would go to college. Many of the younger ones would leave to attend state universities in California. But many more stayed where they were. Some went to community colleges nearby and continued to work at the theater part-time. Others did not seek a college education at all. Still others had already completed their stints at community colleges and were working full-time at the theater. I never contemplated their options—ultimately, my grades would grant me choices that my co-workers could never imagine. But back then, we were not all that different, and I was happy to have them in my life.

Around the same time, I started to play tennis. A friend had introduced me to the National Junior Tennis League (NJTL), a program that the late tennis star Arthur Ashe founded to teach tennis to young people who might not otherwise have the opportunity to learn the sport. Each summer, NJTL fanned out across inner-city America, teaching poor kids how to swing a racket, follow tennis etiquette, and respect themselves and their opponents. More importantly, the program offered them a way to stay "off the streets." I had never been "on the streets," but I eagerly showed up for the free lessons, mindful of how expensive the equivalent private lessons would have been. After one summer with the program, I qualified for my high school's tennis team.

When my team traveled to our "away" games, we visited high schools deep in the bowels of inner-city Oakland. These schools' buildings and facilities appeared to be crumbling, and the threat of violence hung in the air. Anger flashed in the students' eyes. The atmosphere felt like that of a war zone, except when a blank stare replaced the flashes of anger, and one was reminded that the war zone offered no future.

In comparison, the part of town in which I lived seemed heavenly. It was dilapidated, dangerous, and disorderly, but it was merely depressing, not hopeless. My parents had made sure that I lived in a house, not in the projects. They worked so that I could be fed and clothed, instead of abandoned on the streets or at a shelter. By the time I was a senior in high school, I drove a used car and never had to contemplate committing crimes that might have landed me in the back of a police vehicle. Life in the inner city was far from ideal for my family, but it could have been much,

much worse.

During an "away" tennis match at one of these schools, I sat on the sidelines and watched two girls play. They were similar in height and build, and played a similar game. The match was drawn-out and competitive. When one of the girls finally lost, she did not hide her disappointment. Dejected, she walked up to the net and barely shook her opponent's hand. Her coach, a middle-aged, slightly overweight man, shouted to her, "Hey, next time you lose, I want you to look your opponent in the eye when you shake her hand. I don't care if you lose, but I need you to keep your head up and remember to look your opponent in the eye. Alright?" His student nodded before she walked away.

I cannot remember if I won or lost my own match later that day, but I never forgot that scene between coach and student. In the middle of the inner city's desperation, a fatherly figure had tried to teach a young girl about respect and sportsmanship. For a moment, I forgot how much I wanted to escape.

The next summer, I continued to play tennis while working at the movie theater. I eagerly attended my college-level English class and enjoyed it immensely. One night, in a compilation of contemporary American essays assigned by my professor, I found one that said: "You do what you do for your love of it. The sky is the limit."

My books, movies, and tennis made the ghetto a more tolerable place to be, but they also reminded me that I had a big world to see and big dreams to pursue. My grades provided the ticket out. When I graduated from high school, I got as far away from the ghetto as I could. After that, the sky was indeed the limit.

Epilogue

I left the ghetto to attend Cornell University in Ithaca, New York. I could not have asked for a more beautiful college campus. There were rolling hills, stunning waterfalls, enchanting gorges, and Gothic architecture.

College offered a whole new set of promises, but for much of my first semester, I could not trust these promises or enjoy my new surroundings. My new world seemed unreal—there was no poverty, no homelessness, and virtually no crime. For the first time, I was living in a place where a majority of the residents were white. I had to adjust to their world, their lingo, their habits, and their culture. They seemed to have endless supplies of cash. During freshman year, my roommate often spent more on pretzels and ginger ale in one week than I did on snacks for a whole semester. My classmates sported brand names I had never heard of, including L.L. Bean, J. Crew, Timberland, The North Face, and Eddie Bauer. I did my shopping at Woolworth's. While I wrote letters home to avoid an expensive long-distance phone bill, most of my fellow students spoke to their families on the phone whenever they pleased. Their interests ranged from the mindless and harmful (alcohol, drugs, and nonstop partying) to the expensive (scuba diving, skiing, music lessons, spring break in Cancun, and dinner outings in town). I observed all of this with curiosity, disgust, and jealousy.

"You have no idea how much I admire your courage to leave home for a university far, far away," wrote my aunt. Just as her letters had once given me the strength to face the horrors of the ghetto, her letters during my college years helped me find the courage to open myself to the new possibilities an Ivy League university offered.

In time, I allowed my bitterness to peel away before the wonders of learning. I fell in love with the silent beauty of Ithaca's first snowfall each winter and the spectacular colors of its changing foliage each fall. I made new friends who helped me discover the joys of pursuing interests that might seem goofy, superficial, or even moronic. I learned to smile in a way that I had never thought I could in the ghetto.

The summer before I graduated from college, I proudly campaigned for Proposition 209, the ballot initiative that ended state-sponsored, race- and gender-based quotas and preferences in California. After Cornell, I attended Stanford Law School, served Fortune 500 clients at one of the country's leading Wall Street law firms, joined the excitement at the first Mainland China-based Internet company to list on the Nasdaq Stock Market, worked for a high-profile congressional commission, and conducted research at prominent conservative think tanks.

I delved into the study of China and got to know it beyond the haziness of my own memories. I wrote about the excitement of its modern transformation, the depths of its repression, and the insidiousness of its government control. Somewhere along the line, I realized that had it not been for the failures of China, my family would never have embarked on our journey to the ghetto.

As the years passed, I lost my aunt in Guangzhou to cancer and my grandparents to old age. Before they passed away, my grandparents had cheered me on from the ghetto, my grandmother vocally and my grandfather silently. On the day Grandma learned I was working for a congressional commission, she beamed and bragged to everyone, "My granddaughter works for Congress." Grandpa did not brag. Instead, he quietly stashed away evidence of my academic or professional achievements, such as pictures of Cornell or local newspaper clippings about my work.

Two years after I graduated from college, my aunt was diagnosed with cancer in her cheekbone. Before her illness began to show visibly, I visited Guangzhou often. As we strolled through the city that had once belonged to me, strangers often asked if I was her daughter. "If only I were so lucky" was always her response. Each time, my smile froze as I remembered that the Chinese government had forcibly taken away her unborn child.

As my aunt's cancer spread, she lost the strength to enjoy Guangzhou with me. Doctors gouged out half of her face and she underwent chemotherapy and radiation. Her hair fell out and she vomited often, but she fought the disease bravely, rallying the strength she had so often shared with my family in our moments of need. Until her last breath, I believed she could and would win. When she did not, I cursed everything that had conspired to take her away before I was ready for her to go. For months after her death, I saw her face every time I looked up at the blue sky or into the open sea.

My parents were still with me, though, and they were still in the ghetto. Over the years, the ghetto persisted in showing me its ugliness, both in Oakland and beyond. Shortly after I graduated from college, I saw a black woman shriek curses at a Korean man on a bus between New York City and Washington, DC. "You f---ing Chinese person! Didn't you hear that I asked you to move your ass? You too stupid to understand English or something?" she berated him. Years later, I saw a black girl yell at the top of her lungs on a Manhattan-bound Number 7 train, "Man, I fucking hate Indian people. They smell, too, because I know they don't wash." Just as in Oakland, those who witnessed these incidents looked away and pretended nothing had happened. More often than not, I joined them in their silence.

At home, however, I could not look away. Each time I returned to Oakland from "fancy" schools or prestigious employers, I observed that my parents continued to live with the gunshots, the theft, the racism, the indignities, the threats, and the fear. And I had to live with the same for the duration of my holidays and vacations. Through its grip on my family, the ghetto clung to me, and each time I smelled its stench, I hated it more.

Even as various other parts of Oakland received facelifts or underwent gentrification, our neighborhood remained crime-ridden. Robbers broke into our house the summer after I graduated from college. I was on a multi-day train ride from Guangzhou to Chengdu in China. Years later, as I studied for the New York Bar Exam, my father made the mistake of driving up to the stop sign by our corner liquor store with his windows rolled down. As his car stopped, a group of teenage girls descended upon him. Several ran to the driver's side of the car to beat him on the head, in the face, and on the shoulders. The rest reached into the passenger's side window and ransacked the glove compartment. My father managed to drive away. He was not knifed, held up at gunpoint, or seriously injured. He had not kept any valuables in the glove compartment, either. The teenage girls returned to their loitering in front of the liquor store. No one confronted or reprimanded them. No one called the police.

During my absences from Oakland, my brother took care of my parents when he himself was not away. He read the letters they could not understand, took them to the emergency room in the middle of the night, helped them dispute everything from mistaken credit card charges to wrongfully issued parking tickets, and answered their questions about the mortgage, the news, and America in general. These tasks weighed on him, just as they weighed on me every time I performed them.

During my sophomore year in college, my mother sustained a permanent injury while working as a machine operator. A colleague accidentally drove over her ankle with a forklift. Years later, when I was in law school, she slipped and fell while working as a janitor, fracturing her wrist and sustaining another permanent injury. While her wrist was wrapped in a cast, her supervisor called to reprimand my mother for not coming to work.

Finally, during my law school years, I told my family that we had to move. I simply could no longer live under the ghetto's reign. So in my late twenties, while learning about the constitutional right to assistance of counsel and the use of force under international law, I spent my free time reliving my high school days by helping my family purchase a house. This time, I had the additional task of helping them sell one, too. Just as I had done in high school, I pored over mountains of paperwork. On the day I graduated from law school, as my classmates attended celebratory lunches and dinners with their families, I sat at the school's bookstore café with my parents, reviewing documents that explained what rights and responsibilities they had gained with their signatures, and readying our family for the closing.

In the end, the day we moved into our new house was the happiest day of my life. Our new house sits on a safe and quiet street in a neighborhood where the grass is green and the birds are chirpy. My parents can take strolls whenever they want to and can plant a garden in the front yard. They can visit our neighbors without fearing that they might steal our belongings or threaten our physical safety. The police patrol our new city aggressively, but mainly to issue traffic tickets and citations for petty crimes.

At long last, our struggle to break away from the

ghetto was over. From Guangzhou to the ghetto, our journey had turned out to be long and arduous, dark and painful, but twenty years after our arrival in America, we were finally free.

Acknowledgements

Peter Berkowitz and Kevin Hassett believed in this book before anyone else did. "I'm going to write a book titled *From Guangzhou to the Ghetto*," I told Peter over brunch in New York's West Village and Kevin at a Thai restaurant in Washington, D.C. As I sketched out a bare-bones plan, they both listened with the curiosity and patience they have bestowed on many of my harebrained ideas. When we were done talking, both of them had pledged their support.

I had no idea how extensive their support would become. Over the next two years, both Peter and Kevin would read and comment on my draft chapters, connect me with literary agents and publishers, listen to me complain about the writing process, and encourage me to persist with my effort. Peter facilitated my affiliation with his employer, the Hoover Institution at Stanford University; Kevin offered suggestions on everything from the structure to the cover to the title of the book. I am grateful for their friendship and their good humor. Additionally, I am honored to have such frequent access to two of the most distinguished conservative scholars I know. I have called upon both of them for advice on professional and intellectual pursuits beyond this book. In particular, I hope that Kevin will continue to entertain my questions about nearly everything under the sun, and I look forward to continuing to cite his research and analysis in my own articles.

David Brady at the Hoover Institution provided me with a visiting fellowship, a grant for research, and enlightening conversations over spicy Chinese food. I could not have asked for a more congenial group of colleagues than those at Hoover. Through a hands-off approach that prizes free thinking over ideological control, Hoover made it possible for my writing to shine.

I was fortunate to have three readers review my manuscript from beginning to end: Russell Berman, who gave me space in the pages and on the website of *Telos* and urged me to stand strong in the face of political correctness in law school and at a premier Wall Street law firm; Rhoda Rabkin, who rescued me from the tediousness of editing a bilingual newsletter at one of my previous jobs and convinced me that fine prose requires not just imagination but also meticulous editing; and a former professor from Cornell who taught me to comply with the edicts issued by the *Chicago Manual of Style* and who insisted that I devote more space in this book to those who had been kind to me in the ghetto. All three of these individuals offered valuable feedback, critiques, and insights that helped improve this book.

My copy editor, Tai West, performed the unenviable task of whipping this book into printable shape.

Her keen eye for detail saved me from numerous potentially embarrassing errors, and her constructive criticism of the book's content forced me to clarify the text. Most of all, I have appreciated, and needed, her unwavering friendship.

The following people read and commented on draft chapters of the book in its infancy and offered keen observations as well as words of encouragement: Ethan Gutmann, Glen Liu, Adam Bellow, Montgomery Brown, and Harry Crocker. Special thanks to Ethan for initiating several multi-hour trans-Atlantic phone conversations to lift my spirits when my frustrations with writing this book mounted.

A number of people offered advice about book writing and shared their contacts in the publishing world: Sheri Annis, my comrade-in-arms from Proposition 209 and this book's tireless champion at every stage; Tod Lindberg, my editor at *Policy Review*, who has offered me space in his magazine for the past decade and paid me the compliment of having high expectations for my work; John Miller, my great resource for everything ranging from job searches to book publication; and Gene Meyer, my sage and friend, and the man to whom every conservative law student owes thanks.

Jim Hoge kindly offered advice on a busy day. Jamie Glazov connected me with a trusted literary agent. Ward Connerly and Xiao Qiang provided great inspiration through their respective crusades—Ward in fighting for racial equality in America and Xiao Qiang in fighting for freedom in China. Kristina Phillips designed a beautiful cover.

Thanks also go to those who stood by me long before I ever contemplated writing this book. My childhood friends in China stand out the most. Amid the ambiguity of authoritarian rule and the ambivalence of living under it, they taught that there was also friendship and loyalty, leadership and defiance.

I would never have made it out of the ghetto intact had it not been for numerous residents of Oakland, including complete strangers, who lent a helping hand, offered a warm smile, and chose decency over hate. I remain friends with Carl Mendoza, who taught me how to play tennis in a sketchy part of Oakland. I regularly tease him for having verbally abused me in my youth, but I am grateful to him for continuing to teach inner-city children the values of hard work, discipline, and self-respect through the great sport of tennis.

I wish my grandparents could have been alive to see this book. As the intellectual of my family, my grandfather was always in a unique position to understand my academic pursuits, including those that did not make any financial sense. My grandmother, a wise and practical woman, understood my abilities from a very different vantage point and never hesitated to vocalize her faith in them. I miss them and my late aunt. Together with my immediate family, they made it possible for me to marvel at the wonders of childhood in China, and reminded me, even in the ghastliness of the ghetto, of the happiness I once held—and could grasp again.

Finally, I owe an insurmountable debt to my parents and my brother for having traveled with me from

Guangzhou to the ghetto. No words can adequately describe the sacrifice that my parents made or the doggedness with which my brother believed that his little sister could one day make something of herself. These pages offer mere glimpses of what my family has done for me and what it took for us to scratch, claw, and kick our way to a better life in America. For that reason, this book is dedicated to them.

About the Author

Ying Ma is a visiting fellow at the Hoover Institution on War, Revolution and Peace at Stanford University. She writes about China, Asia, U.S. foreign policy, and racial politics in America. Her work has appeared in *The Christian Science Monitor*, the *International Herald Tribune*, the *Los Angeles Times*, *Policy Review*, National Review Online, *The Wall Street Journal Asia*, *The Washington Times,* and other publications. She immigrated to the United States from China at age ten. She is a term member of the Council on Foreign Relations.

CPSIA information can be obtained at www.ICGtesting.com
Printed in the USA
244118LV00001B/22/P